Labour Management, Contracts and Capital Markets

Yrjö Waldemar Jahnsson, 1877–1936, was Professor of Economics at the Institute of Technology, Helsinki. In 1954, his wife Hilma Jahnsson established, in accordance with her husband's wishes, a foundation. The specific purpose of the Yrjö Jahnsson Foundation is to promote economic research in Finland. To this end the Foundation supports the work of individual scholars and institutions by awarding them scholarships and grants. It also invites internationally renowned economists to Finland to give courses of lectures which are then published in this series.

YRJÖ JAHNSSON LECTURES

Kenneth J. Arrow
Aspects of the Theory of Risk-Bearing

Assar Lindbeck
Monetary-Fiscal Analysis and General Equilibrium

L. R. Klein
An Essay on the Theory of Economic Prediction

Harry G. Johnson
The Two-Sector Model of General Equilibrium

John Hicks
The Crisis in Keynesian Economics

E. Malinvaud
The Theory of Unemployment Reconsidered

James Tobin
Asset Accumulation and Economic Activity

János Kornai
Growth, Shortage and Efficiency

Robert E. Lucas, Jr
Models of Business Cycles

Yrjö Jahnsson Lectures

Labour Management, Contracts and Capital Markets

A General Equilibrium Approach

JACQUES H. DRÈZE

Basil Blackwell

First published 1989

Basil Blackwell Ltd
108 Cowley Road, Oxford, OX4 1JF, UK

Basil Blackwell Inc.
432 Park Avenue South, Suite 1503
New York, NY 10016, USA

British Library Cataloguing in Publication Data

Drèze, Jacques, H., 1929–
Labour management, contracts and capital
markets: a general equilibrium approach.
— (Yrjö Jahnsson lectures).
1. Econometric models. Applications of
general equilibrium theory
I. Title II. Series
330′.0724
ISBN 0-631-13784-X

Library of Congress Cataloging in Publication Data

Drèze, Jacques H.
Labour management, contracts, and capital markets: a general
equilibrium approach / Jacques H. Drèze.
p. cm. — (Yrjö Jahnsson lectures)
Bibliography: p. Includes index.
ISBN 0-631.13784-X
1. Equilibrium (Economics) 2. Uncertainty. 3. Management-
Employee participation. 4. Stock market. 5. Labor contract.
I. Title. II. Series.
HB145.D74 1989
658.3′15—dc19

Typeset in 10 on 12pt Times, by Colset Pte Ltd, Singapore
Printed in Great Britain by
Billing & Sons Ltd, Worcester

Contents

To our sons Benoit
Jean
Pascal
Xavier
François

wishing them to experience self-management in a full-employment society

Preface

This is a revised version of the manuscript initially prepared for the 1983 Yrjö Jahnsson Lectures. Delivering these lectures in Helsinki was a very pleasant experience, thanks to the hospitality extended by many Finnish economists, in particular Vesa Kanniainen, Timo Terasvirta and Esko Vuorela.

Needless to say, the oral lectures were less technical and less detailed than the manuscript. I have made some effort to keep technical developments out of the main text. Consequently, the more original material is buried in the appendices. Holding the manuscript for revisions enabled me to include appendices 3 and 5, and to rewrite chapters 3 and 5. A slightly more explicit title was also chosen.

Several friends and colleagues have given me the benefit of their suggestions. I am particularly grateful to Jean Dermine, Bengt Holmström, James Malcomson, Jack Mintz and Jan Svejnar for their written comments.

The successive versions of the manuscript were prepared with competence and dedication by Ginette Vincent. I am very grateful to her. I also thank the Yrjö Jahnsson Foundation and Basil Blackwell for their patience.

Introduction and Preview

Human labour and economic theory

This book brings together a set of ideas, and a few analytical results, reflecting my growing concern over the past fifteen years with some implications of the simple observation that human labour is not just another commodity, like cashew nuts, transistor radios or automobile windshields. At a common sense level, that observation hardly requires elaboration. Radios do not care whether they are turned off, relay news items or disseminate music. Human beings care whether they are employed or not, whether their work is useful, pleasant and so on. But my concern here is not with common sense, it is with economic theory. For many years, when lecturing on general equilibrium theory, I had commented cursorily: 'Among the ℓ commodities, we find different types of labour as well as physical goods or services; there is no theoretical need to distinguish these two kinds of commodities.' For most purposes, that approach is satisfactory because human beings enter the theory as consumers, endowed with subjective preferences defined over the work which they perform as well as the goods or services which they consume. But there are limitations, sometimes due to our practice, sometimes inherent in the approach. Indeed, our practice often stops at the simpler and more elegant models, where significant imperfections of the real world are suppressed. For instance, we may ignore specific market failures associated with uncertainty or with price rigidities. Or we may model uncertainty and incomplete markets in a way which neglects the firm-specific components of human capital. Such practices are amenable to improvement within the traditional approach. But other limitations are not due to oversimplification in our use of the model; they are rooted in the design of the model itself. Thus, preferences of worker-consumers for the design of organizations, for the definition of labour conditions (the definition of commodities) or for the set of individuals with whom they work require fundamental modifications of the theoretical model. Existing theories are of little help in accommodating such phenomena.

This work remains theoretical in nature, reflecting my conviction that a proper understanding of the economic problems associated with the unique features of human labour is likely to be enhanced by careful theorizing as well as by more informal approaches. The theoretical bias entails severe limitations, however, as I shall leave out such paramount issues as the direct impact of work organization on welfare and on productivity. My excuse for these omissions is ignorance. But there would be no excuse for failing to turn those tools over which I have some command in a direction which I regard as important, promising and insufficiently explored. The tools used here are those of general equilibrium theory in the three main forms currently in use, namely competitive equilibrium, temporary equilibrium and constrained equilibrium.

Labour management

A theme which has retained my lasting attention, and the first to be developed in this book, is that of labour management, understood somewhat narrowly as a form of economic organization where production decisions are made collectively by the workers taking part in the production process. This is a very natural theme for an academic to consider, since he operates in an environment – the university – where *professors* enjoy a large degree of collective (and individual) autonomy.

The economic theory of labour management has concentrated mostly on the operating characteristics of production units (firms) aiming at maximization of the individual incomes of workers. The criterion of 'value added per worker' is thus substituted for the profit criterion.

A major source of inspiration for that work has come from Yugoslavia, where production is by and large labour managed. A number of more limited experiences are commonly cited, including the Soviet farms, the Israeli kibbutzim, the Spanish cooperative at Mondragon, and various isolated case histories in industrialized countries (see part 3 of Vanek 1975 for an account). In recent years, attempts at continuation on a labour-managed basis of European firms threatened with bankruptcy has drawn some attention, for instance at the French watch factory Lipp.

Labour management is a useful paradigm to study economic decisions in at least three additional sets of circumstances:

(i) Some public utilities, operating under legal monopoly protection, seem to achieve for their employees rates of pay and/or fringe benefits more favourable than local market alternatives. Their behaviour is perhaps better captured through the 'value added per worker' criterion than through alternative criteria like profit, social welfare and so on.
(ii) Small business ventures owned and operated by members of a family (farms, vineyards, stores, fishing boats, garages and the like) also come close to the labour-management model.
(iii) Labour unions are often depicted as promoting the interests of the workers at present employed in a given firm or industrial sector (as distinct from the workers at large, or the general public).[1] Their goal could then be understood as that of enforcing (upon capitalist firms) the very decisions that workers themselves would reach under labour management.

I shall thus be concerned with the economic theory of labour management, not only for its own sake, but also for the lessons which can be drawn regarding some aspects of capitalist or mixed economies. In that spirit, it is of interest to study labour management from a general equilibrium viewpoint: first, to check the overall consistency of that model of production; and second, to investigate its compatibility, or absence of compatibility, with other forms of organization. Such is the subject of chapter 1. After defining a labour-management equilibrium, I present an equivalence theorem: the sets of allocations that can be sustained as labour-management equilibria, or as competitive equilibria, are identical. That result brings the well-developed theory of competitive equilibria to bear on labour management. It also establishes the compatibility of different forms of organization within a given market economy – at no loss in efficiency.

Labour contracts and capital markets

A second theme, which figures prominently in this book, concerns the interaction of labour and capital in the more realistic setting of uncertainty with incomplete insurance markets. In that setting, firms must decide about their investments, production and employment plans without finding in market prices unambiguous signals regarding the value of these plans. Yet decide they must, and their decisions have important consequences for the welfare of households, which are concerned as investors owning the firms, as workers supplying the labour inputs, and as consumers purchasing the output.

The theory of finance has been concerned with the dual role of capital markets in bringing about efficient risk-sharing among investors and in providing firms with information about the risk preferences of these investors. But workers are also concerned with production and investment decisions, because their human capital is at stake, and because the main component of their income comes from wages (or profit shares) which are also subject to uncertainties.

Thus, the consequences of the decisions of firms for the human capital of their workers should be taken into account as much as the consequences for the capital supplied by investors. And efficient risk-sharing should encompass not only the property income of investors but also the labour income of workers. Understandably, these aspects are not properly covered in the theory of finance.

New light has been thrown on these topics by the recent development of a theory of labour contracts, in a setting of uncertainty with incomplete markets – a development often referred to as 'implicit contracts theory'.[2]

Chapters 2 and 3 present an integration of the approaches of the theories of finance and of labour contracts, in a general equilibrium framework. The decisions of firms are modelled in a more realistic way than is usual in general equilibrium theory, allowing for control by a board of directors subject to approval by majority voting of shareholders on the one hand, and for negotiations between the firm and workers regarding labour contracts on the other. Also, the implications of the pricing of capital assets for efficient labour contracts are considered.

That material naturally paves the way for a discussion of the financial structure of labour-managed firms in chapter 4. The need for equity financing is readily recognized, leading once more to an equivalence property, as well as to a sharper understanding of the major obstacle limiting the development of labour-managed firms in the capital-intensive sectors of private ownership economies (namely, insufficient access to equity financing). A fuller explanation of that limited development is suggested in chapter 5, namely that organized labour can direct its efforts more fruitfully towards improving the terms of labour contracts than the terms on which labour-managed firms could raise equity capital. That explanation had not occurred to me before, and came out of this work.

Economy-wide wage settlements

A third theme, in which my interest is more recent, concerns economy-wide wage settlements and the trade-off between labour incomes and employment. That theme was not covered in the oral lectures, but it seemed natural to introduce it briefly at the end of this book, for the following reason. While revising the manuscript, I realized that the standard empirical model of the theory of finance, namely the Capital Asset Pricing Model (CAPM), suggests economy-wide wage settlements as a natural avenue towards efficient risk-sharing between capital and labour. Interestingly, the realization came from reviewing the characterization of efficient labour contracts at the firm level, in the general equilibrium setting of chapter 3. In the CAPM framework the shareholders of all firms are the same, so that wage settlements have no reason to be firm specific, as a first approximation. Economy-wide settlements, which are of central relevance in macroeconomics, thus emerge as a natural implication of microeconomic analysis.

Like implicit contracts models, the general equilibrium model of chapter 3 does not associate wasteful unemployment with wage rigidities. The reason is that contracts provide a framework for reconciling risk-sharing with productive efficiency. On the other hand, future generations of workers are not covered by forward labour contracts. For them, downward wage rigidity is conducive to wasteful unemployment; it is also a form of income protection which carries a risk-sharing feature. This raises an issue of second-best efficiency, in balancing the output losses due to unemployment against the risk-sharing gains due to wage stability. Looking at that issue in a framework where older generations are covered by efficient labour contracts is intriguing. A first step in that direction, based upon work posterior to the oral lectures (see appendix 5), concludes this book on a theme of genuine significance for policy as well as research. It is also a theme which blends naturally into my concise overall conclusion at the end of chapter 5.

Notes

1 'Insider-outsider theories' of wages and employment are a case in point; see for example Lindbeck and Snower (1985) and the references given there.

2 The Finnish economist Bengt Holmström (1983), among others, has contributed significantly to that development; see also Hart and Holmström (1988) for more recent references.

CHAPTER 1

Labour-managed Market Economies

1.1 Introduction

Two views of labour management

An economist's interest in labour management may have two main origins.[1] First, most human beings prefer to have a say in decisions regarding the activities in which they are personally involved. This principle underlying political democracy is even more relevant in the economic sphere, especially with regard to production activities in which human beings are physically and psychologically involved. The term 'industrial democracy' is sometimes used to describe an organization of production activities where decisions are vested with those personally involved; in short, where labour management prevails. Although collective decision-making is apt to be time consuming, and sometimes conducive to conflicts which deteriorate working relationships, there is little doubt in my mind that the quest for self-determination is deep rooted in human psychology. Denial of this natural aspiration is bound to create frustrations, feelings of alienation and conflicts. (Life at a university is as telling in this respect as life at a factory, an office or a farm.) Accordingly, it is a question of great interest for economics to investigate whether, and possibly under what conditions, industrial democracy through labour management can be a *workable* system and an *economically efficient* one. Needless to say, the question is a difficult one; it has many aspects which are not encompassed by the discipline of economics; and it has aspects on which theory alone could throw little light, if unaided by empirical analysis of historical experiences.

There are, however, many decisions of relevance to a person's activities in which he or she cannot participate effectively: either because the decisions are so numerous that some delegation of authority is indispensable for expediency; or because the problems are so technical and complex that specialized training is needed to comprehend them. In these circumstances, reasonable persons will prefer not to participate directly in the decision-making process. Instead, they will delegate authority to specialists. Yet, they will want some assurance that their interests are duly taken into account, so that decisions made by the specialists are in agreement with those which they would themselves reach, given proper information and training. Here lies the second origin of interest of an economist in labour management. We wish to investigate whether, and possibly under what circumstances, decisions regarding production activities at a level quite remote from the shop floor (for instance, decisions regarding product mixes, selling prices, investment or finances) *conform to the aspirations* of the human beings ultimately involved. This second line of investigation differs from the first, in that it abstracts from the decision-making process itself to concentrate on its outcome – the decisions reached. This confines the question more narrowly to economic aspects, and even to those aspects which theory is more specifically designed to clarify. Indeed, it has been the central concern of economic theory to study the decisions of households, producers or policy-makers, and their consequences for the welfare of human beings in their triple capacity as consumers, workers and asset owners.

In the pursuit of that concern, little explicit attention had been paid, until quite recently, to the possible implications of a form of organization under which producers' decisions are governed *by the interests* of the workers carrying out the production activities. The economic theory of labour-managed market economies, to which important contributions have been made over the past thirty years, aims at filling that gap.

Labour-managed market economies

The theory deals with an economy where physical commodities are allocated through markets. Labour services are not rented out against a wage or salary. Instead, all production activities are carried out in workers' cooperatives, that is labour-managed firms. These firms borrow financial capital, or rent physical capital equipment, buy additional inputs and produce commodities for sale on the market. Value added, net of the cost of all non-labour inputs, is divided among the workers. The cooperative is assumed to maximize the earnings (so defined) of an individual worker; that is, it maximizes 'value added per worker'.

That model of a labour-managed market economy seems to have been analysed formally for the first time by Benjamin Ward (1958) and Evsey Domar (1966) at the partial equilibrium level of a single firm bringing together a number of identical workers. Their analysis was considerably extended by Jaroslav Vanek, whose *General Theory of Labour-Managed Market Economies* (1970) provided the first comprehensive coverage of the subject. Interest in the book was further stimulated through the excellent review article by James Meade (1972). Over the past fifteen years an abundant literature has developed; the references at the end of this book do not aim at comprehensiveness.[2]

Most of that literature retains 'maximization of value added per worker' as the basic operating characteristic of labour-managed firms. A few papers have extended the criterion to consider the possibility of layoffs or unemployment: see Miyazaki and Neary (1983), Sapir (1980), Spinnewyn (1981) or Steinherr and Thisse (1979). I shall return to that topic in chapter 4.[3]

Outline of the chapter

My programme for this chapter is first to present and motivate a general definition of value added per worker; next to introduce and motivate a general equilibrium concept for a labour-managed market economy; and finally to comment on the three specific issues of capital rents, income distribution and working conditions. The discussion is conducted in the standard framework of general equilibrium theory, namely a framework of complete certainty with a full set of markets.[4] Extensions to uncertainty with incomplete markets, and to non-clearing markets, will be taken up in chapter 4.

1.2 Value added per worker

Homogeneous labour and fixed membership

Value added per worker is a straightforward concept in the case of a firm bringing together a set of identical workers in a market economy.

Denote by $y = (y_1, \ldots, y_g, \ldots, y_G)$ the vector of physical inputs or outputs which, together with some quantity z of a single labour input, define a production plan for the firm. The technological possibilities open to the firm are defined by a set Y in R^{G+1}, the space of physical goods and labour. Thus (y, z) is feasible if and only if (y, z) belongs to Y. As usual, negative components of y denote inputs and positive components denote outputs. If the market prices of physical goods are taken as given and denoted by $p = (p_1, \ldots, p_g, \ldots, p_G)$, then the scalar product

$$py = \sum_{g=1}^{G} p_g y_g$$

is the market value of *net* output or value added. This value added is defined gross of labour earnings but net of *all* other costs.

I shall refer later to the specific problems associated with capital – either physical or financial – or with time and discounting. It is easier to think first in terms of a single period, with instantaneous production and no durable inputs (as when physical capital goods are leased). I thus depart provisionally from the conventional definition, which considers value added gross of capital outlays.

The problem faced by the members of the firm is to choose y and z, with (y, z) belonging to given Y. Considering first a fixed value of z, say $\bar{z}$, it seems reasonable to assume that y will be chosen so as to maximize py subject to $(y, \bar{z})$ in Y. Given the fixed value $\bar{z}$, this choice maximizes the aggregate earnings which the members of the firm will share among themselves. If sales and purchases of physical goods at prices p are unrestricted, it is difficult to think of any compelling reason for deviating from this choice. (For instance, there is no reason for the workers to let their own consumption preferences interfere with this choice, since they can always satisfy their consumption needs through market purchases – the better so, the higher is their disposable income.) I use $y(\bar{z})$ as an abbreviated notation for $y(\bar{z}, p)$, the chosen vector of inputs and outputs.

What can we say about the choice of $\bar{z}$? If the firm consisted of a fixed, given membership of *n identical workers* with no alternative employment opportunities (as in the case of an isolated village of fixed population with a single firm), these workers would each perform a quantity of work $\bar{z}/n$; and it would seem natural to assume equal sharing of the value added. (The 'identical workers' assumption may be understood to imply identical family compositions and needs, for the time being.) Thus each worker would supply a quantity of labour $\bar{z}/n$ and earn an income py/n.

The natural tendency of the economist would next be to assume that workers have well-defined (identical) preferences for combinations of working time (hence leisure) and disposable income. Letting these preferences be represented by a utility function, as permitted by standard assumptions, write $u(py/n, z/n)$ for the utility level of an individual worker. It will then be natural for the workers to choose z so as to maximize $u(py(z)/n, z/n)$. A simple graphical representation of this problem is given in figure 1. In drawing this simple and familiar figure, advantage is taken of the fact that value added per worker, $py(z)/n$, is a scalar function of z for given p and n; whereas a worker's preferences are unambiguously defined in terms of that quantity and z/n for given p. The optimal choice corresponds to point a in the figure (which is drawn for a convex production set and convex preferences).

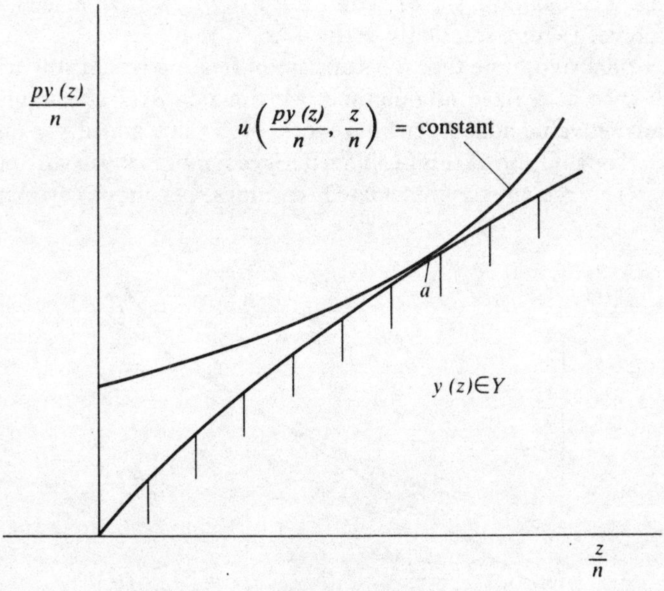

Figure 1

Variable membership, identical tastes

Point a in figure 1 does not maximize value added per worker; it maximizes each worker's utility level. In order to bring in value added per worker, a different set of circumstances must be considered. Instead of starting from a fixed membership, assume instead that the quantity of labour to be supplied by each member is fixed, but the number of members is variable. (For instance, the length of the working week is a legal datum; the firm is to bring together a group of workers who will resign from their current salaried employment to form a cooperative.)

In this second case, $z/n = \bar{\ell}$ (say), a fixed quantity. Writing $y(n)$ for $y(z|z = n\bar{\ell})$, a worker's utility level becomes $u(py(n)/n,\ \bar{\ell})$. Maximization of this level through choice of n reduces to maximization, with respect to n, of $py(n)/n$, which is precisely value added per worker. In this way, the decision by the workers reduces to finding the point (y, z) in the production set Y where $py(z)/(z/\bar{\ell})(= py(n)/n)$ is maximal. Note furthermore that $\bar{\ell}$ plays no role in this calculation, since maximization of $py(z)/z$ would lead to the same choice (with n implicitly defined as $z/\bar{\ell}$).

As a final step, note that the same simplification would still arise in the absence of a fixed labour time. Maximizing $py(z)/z$ amounts to maximizing value added per hour worked or value added per unit of labour. The solution of this problem defines simultaneously an optimal input level z and the associated earnings per hour $py(z)/z$. A

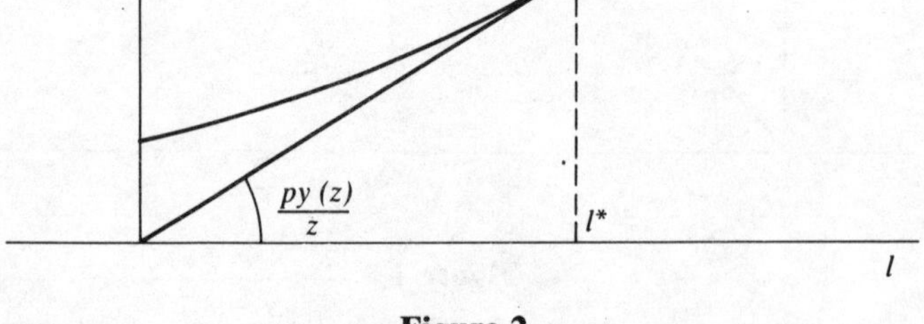

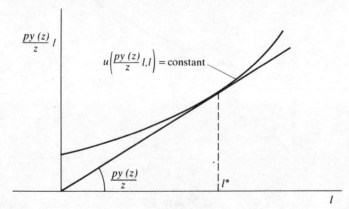

Figure 2

prospective member of the firm could then choose his own labour supply ℓ by computing the associated earnings $\ell py(z)/z$ and utility level $u(\ell py(z)/z, \ell)$. His or her maximization problem, with solution ℓ^*, is depicted in figure 2, which is again familiar from the analysis of labour supply.

In this third case, the number of members of the firm is determined in two steps. An abstract calculation defines the maximal level of value added per hour worked $py(z)/z$ attained at some level of labour input z^* (measured in hours). Each identical worker defines *on that basis* his or her preferred labour supply ℓ^*. There results a membership size $n^* = z^*/\ell^*$.

When all commodity prices are given, so that py is a well-defined scalar, and

$$py(z) = \max_y py \qquad \text{subject to } (y, z) \in Y$$

is a well-defined function of z, two situations should be distinguished according to whether $py(z)$ is, or is not, a concave function of z. Convexity of the production set Y entails that the function $py(z)$ is concave in z for fixed p.[5]

To say that $py(z)$ is a concave function of z is to say that value added per hour worked is a non-increasing function of labour input z, when the production set Y contains the origin (possibility of inaction).

Proof Writing $f(z)$ for $py(z)$, concavity means

$$f(z) \leqslant f(z_0) + (z - z_0)\,\nabla f(z_0) \tag{1.1}$$

where $\nabla f(z_0) \geqslant 0$ is any element of the subgradient of f at z_0. Applying this inequality with $z = 0$, we have

$$z_0 \nabla f(z_0) - f(z_0) \leqslant -f(0) \leqslant 0. \tag{1.2}$$

For $z \neq 0$, we may divide through by z in (1.1), obtaining

$$\frac{f(z)}{z} \leqslant \frac{f(z_0)}{z} + \frac{z - z_0}{z}\,\nabla f(z_0). \tag{1.3}$$

For $z_0 \neq 0$, the right-hand side of (1.3) is equal to

$$\frac{f(z_0)}{z_0} + \left[\frac{f(z_0)}{z} - \frac{f(z_0)}{z_0}\right] + \frac{z - z_0}{z}\,\nabla f(z_0)$$

$$= \frac{f(z_0)}{z_0} + \frac{f(z_0)(z_0 - z) + z_0(z - z_0)\nabla f(z_0)}{z_0 z} \tag{1.4}$$

$$= \frac{f(z_0)}{z_0} + \frac{z - z_0}{z_0 z}[z_0 \nabla f(z_0) - f(z_0)]$$

$$\gtreqless \frac{f(z_0)}{z_0} \quad \text{as } z \lesseqgtr z_0,$$

in view of (1.2). Thus

$$\frac{f(z)}{z} \leqslant \frac{f(z_0)}{z_0} \quad \text{for all } z \geqslant z_0 > 0. \tag{1.5}\Box$$

This case leads to two possibilities. Either $py(z)$ is strictly concave at $z = 0$, in which case $py(z)/z$ is strictly decreasing there and does not attain a maximum for any $z > 0$. Or $py(z)$ is linear in z for $0 \leqslant z \leqslant \hat{z} \leqslant \infty$, in which case $py(z)/z$ attains a maximum over the whole interval $(0, \hat{z})$. This second possibility corresponds to constant returns to labour over the (possibly infinite) range $(0, \hat{z})$. Value added per hour worked is then well defined, but labour input is to some extent indeterminate.

The first possibility – strictly decreasing returns to labour – suggests that the firm is using some non-marketed scarce input. The combination of this specific factor with increasing quantities of all other inputs (including labour) results in decreasing returns. If this non-marketed input were divisible and replicable, then production would best be carried out by an infinity of infinitesimally small firms, and we would be back to constant returns. If it is a scarce, *non-replicable* input, then it would seem reasonable to impute a rent r for its use,[6] and to compute value added as $py(z) - r$ whenever $y(z) \neq 0$, thus defining

$$f(z) \overset{\text{def}}{=} \begin{cases} 0 & z = 0 \\ py(z) - r & z > 0. \end{cases} \tag{1.6}$$

This is a special case of the second situation to be considered, namely that where $f(z)$ is not concave. If $py(z)$ is bounded above, and if there exists z such that $py(z) > r$, then $f(z)/z$ will attain a maximum for some positive, finite z^*. If the function $py(z)$ is differentiable in z at z^*, then z^* is characterized by

$$\left.\frac{d[f(z)/z]}{dz}\right|_{z^*} = 0 \qquad \left.\frac{d^2[f(z)/z]}{dz^2}\right|_{z^*} \leqslant 0. \tag{1.7}$$

These two conditions are readily translated into

$$\frac{py(z^*) - r}{z^*} = p \left.\frac{dy(z)}{dz}\right|_{z^*} \qquad \left.\frac{d^2py(z)}{dz^2}\right|_{z^*} \leqslant 0. \tag{1.8}$$

That is, at the optimum, value added per hour worked is equal to the marginal value product of labour $f'(z) = py'(z)$, and the function $f(z)$ is locally concave. These conditions are readily extended to the non-differentiable case in terms of generalized gradients or directional derivatives – but I shall have no recurrent use for these more technical concepts here.

To sum up, value added per hour worked is a well-defined concept whenever Y displays either constant returns to scale or strict convexity. In the latter case, a positive rent must be imputed for use of the non-marketed input hidden behind the production set. In general, value added may be defined as

$$\max \left[0, \frac{py(z) - r}{z}\right],$$

with $z \geqslant 0$, $r = 0$ in the case of constant returns. (When $z = 0$, the firm does not exist.)

It is important to remember that this formulation rests on the understanding that each member of the firm supplies either a predetermined number of work hours, or a number of work hours of his or her choice. The number of members is implicitly determined as that which is required to attain the desired level of labour input (namely the level which maximizes value added per hour worked); availability of potential members is assumed adequate.

Variable membership, diverse tastes

If we retain the assumption of a single homogeneous labour input, we may allow for diversity of tastes among the workers and let each member of the firm decide individually how many hours he or she cares to supply, it being understood that his or her share in value added will be proportional to the number of hours worked. (Practical considerations relating to the organization of the work flow, or to transportation of the workers, may place some constraints on individual working times, especially when the work is carried out in teams whose working hours need to be coordinated.)

If member i supplies z^i hours, then $\Sigma_i z^i = z$ and the income of member i is $z^i[py(z) - r]/z$. It is still in the interest of every member to maximize earnings per hour, so that the optimal choice of z is the same as before.

Heterogeneous labour: sharing value added

The case of a single homogeneous labour input is quite special. In general, several types of labour inputs need to be considered. They will differ according to the qualifications required (bricklaying or accounting), the type of work performed (carrying logs or carrying teacups), the timing (working the day shift or the night shift), and so on.

Pending further comments in section 1.6, I shall assume the existence of L *given* types of labour. Let then $z = (z_1, \ldots, z_\ell, \ldots, z_L)$ denote a vector of labour inputs. The technological possibilities open to the firm are now defined by a set Y in $R^G \times R^L_+$, the space of physical goods y and labour inputs z. And (y, z) is a feasible production plan if and only if (y, z) belongs to Y – it being understood that different product mixes typically require different mixes of labour inputs.

Value added gross of labour earnings is still defined as py. For a fixed vector of labour inputs $\bar{z}$, quantities of physical goods y may still be chosen to maximize py subject to $(y, \bar{z})$ in Y – yielding a solution $y(\bar{z})$ with value added $py(\bar{z})$. Assume provisionally that membership in the firm is given, and that the total amount $\bar{z}_\ell$ of each type of work ℓ has been apportioned among the members. How will they share the proceeds, $py(\bar{z})$ or $py(\bar{z}) - r$?

The principle advanced in the previous section suggests equal shares per hour of each given type of labour. But what about different types of labour? Should the share (per hour) of a bricklayer be the same as that of an accountant? Should it be the same as that of an apprentice, of an unskilled labourer or of a foreman? Should work on the day shift and on the night shift give rights to equal shares?

This is undoubtedly a difficult question, one that may give rise to much argument among the members, and one that historically has received quite diverse solutions.[7] One point is clear: it would be exceedingly restrictive to assume that all types of labour give right to identical (per hour) shares in value added. That uniformity is not always found in practical experience. And it is intuitively obvious that it could only be maintained in special circumstances, like those of a kibbutz, where members are kept together by ideological bonds, or those of a kolkhoz, where they are kept together by a political authority. Selfish motivations would not lead any member to volunteer for the less attractive types of work (like work on the night shift) if there existed more pleasant but equally rewarded alternatives for which he qualifies.

As soon as this aspect is recognized, one is led to admit some weighting of hours by types of work for the purpose of dividing value added among the members. Let then a_ℓ denote the weight assigned to one hour of labour type ℓ, and normalize the weights by setting $\min_\ell a_\ell = 1$. The total weighted labour input is then $z_w = \Sigma_{\ell=1}^{L} a_\ell z_\ell$. This may be called a total number of equivalent hours, suggesting that one hour of type ℓ labour is 'equivalent' to a_ℓ hours of 'simple' labour. Value added per unit of labour (per hour of simple labour) is then by definition equal to $[py(z) - r]/\Sigma_\ell a_\ell z_\ell$. If member i supplies z_ℓ^i hours of type ℓ labour, $\ell = 1, \ldots, L$, $\Sigma_i z_\ell^i = z_\ell$, then i's income will be $\Sigma_\ell a_\ell z_\ell^i$ $[py(z) - r]/\Sigma_\ell a_\ell z_\ell$ and the sum of incomes over all members will be $py(z) - r$, as desired.

Such an approach seems inescapable. Of course, it does not rule out equality of the a_ℓ if the members so decide. And there remains to discuss what constraints, if any, are imposed on the choice of weights – a point clarified in sections 1.3 and 1.5. In passing, I may note that the existence of such weights is not ruled out by the Marxian labour theory of value, where it is recognized that 'indirect labour' – for instance, time spent on training and the acquisition of knowledge – must be imputed. A concept of equivalent units of simple labour fits into that framework as well, with the weights a_ℓ determined within the theory.

Heterogeneous labour: choosing labour inputs

Assuming at this point that labour weights a_ℓ have been agreed upon, and that members will be free to decide how many hours of each type of labour they will supply (thereby determining membership size endogenously as in the previous section), we may address the question: how many hours of each type of labour will the firm decide to use?

The criterion of maximal value added per unit of labour now calls for solving

$$\max_{(y,z)\in Y} \frac{py - r}{\sum_\ell a_\ell z_\ell} = \text{def } V. \tag{1.9}$$

Indeed, if the workers wish to maximize their earnings per hour worked then, under given weights $a = (a_1, \ldots, a_L)$, maximization of V simultaneously maximizes hourly earnings $a_\ell V$ in every type of work. The solution of problem (1.9) simultaneously determines the quantities of all goods to be produced or used as inputs, and the quantities of all types of labour to be used as inputs (subject to the single constraint of technological feasibility).

Properties of a solution to problem (1.9) are again easily stated and understood in the differentiable case. Let $py(z)$ denote the value added, gross of rent, obtained for given z by maximizing py subject to (y, z) in Y; and let y be a differentiable function of its vector argument z. Then a necessary condition for a solution to (1.9) at z^* is

$$0 = \left.\frac{\partial[(py(z) - r)/\Sigma_\ell a_\ell z_\ell]}{\partial z_k}\right|_{z^*} \qquad k = 1, \ldots, L. \tag{1.10}$$

Writing again $f(z)$ for $py(z)$, we find

$$\frac{\dfrac{\partial f}{\partial z_k}\sum_\ell a_\ell z_\ell - a_k[f(z) - r]}{(\Sigma_\ell a_\ell z_\ell)^2} = 0 \qquad \frac{\partial f}{\partial z_k} = a_k V. \tag{1.11}$$

Here, $\partial f/\partial z_k = \partial py(z)/\partial z_k$ is the marginal value product of one hour of type k labour; $a_k V$ is the hourly earnings for labour type k. Condition (1.11) reveals that each type of labour should be used in such a quantity that its unit share in value added be equal to its marginal value product. (Note that with a single type of labour this condition reduces to the first part of (1.8).) This condition should hold identically in the numerical values of $a_1, \ldots, a_L$; it is a property of efficient use of labour, in the common interest of the firm's members, once they have agreed on a sharing scheme.[8]

We may thus look at the weights $a_1, \ldots, a_L$ as determining simultaneously the *rules of income formation* and the *demand for labour* of all types by the firm. This duality of roles is analogous to that performed by prices in competitive economies. The reasoning here is that all members of an open-ended labour-managed firm will agree to expand (contract) the use of type k labour whenever its marginal value product exceeds (falls short of) $a_k V$, thereby raising V and hence everybody's income. As long as the supplied quantity z^i_ℓ of each labour type ℓ is freely chosen by each member i, he or she can only benefit from the increase in V. As indicated earlier, this reasoning would need to be amended if the membership of the firm were predetermined and the labour input requirements were to be apportioned among members. Quantities of labour inputs would then be determined by the preferences of workers over income and the different types of work.

Supply and demand for labour

Once it is recognized that the rent r and the weights $a_1, \ldots, a_L$ determine not only the incomes of the firm's members but also the total use by the firm of the different types of labour, one is led to wonder about the matching of supply and demand for the different types of labour. In a capitalist market economy, one thinks about prices, including wages and salaries, as adjusting so as to clear all markets. In a labour-managed market economy, prices of physical commodities still serve that function. But there are no prices, in the ordinary sense of the word, to equate supply and demand for the different types of labour. Shares in value added may serve that function, however. One is thus led to define a general equilibrium concept for the labour-managed market economy; this is a task to which I now turn.

1.3 General equilibrium

Labour-management equilibria

On the basis of the discussion in the previous section, we may approach as follows the problem of defining a general equilibrium concept for a labour-managed market economy. There exists a set of firms, to be indexed $j = 1, \ldots, J$. Each firm is characterized by a production set Y^j in $R^G \times R^L_+$, the space of physical commodities and labour types. Some of these firms, say the first K, may use specific scarce inputs, corresponding to existing plants and equipments, on which are imputed rents r^j, $j = 1, \ldots, K$. The remaining firms use only the general technology, characterized by constant returns to scale, and buy all their primary imputs. Their imputed rents are equal to zero. Each firm j chooses a production plan (y^j, z^j) in Y^j. The physical commodities are traded at market prices p (in R^G). The value added for firm j is thus $py^j - r^j, j = 1, \ldots, J$, with $r^j = 0$ for $j = K+1, \ldots, J$.

Each firm j decides on a set of weights $(a_1^j, \ldots, a_L^j)$, with $\min_\ell a_\ell^j = 1$, on the basis of which its value added is to be shared among the members. Thus value added per unit of labour is defined in firm j as

$$V^j = \frac{py^j - r^j}{\sum_{\ell=1}^{L} a_\ell^j z_\ell^j} \tag{1.12}$$

and one hour of labour type ℓ gives right to an income share $a_\ell^j V^j$, $\ell = 1, \ldots, L$. This sharing rule satisfies identically

$$\sum_{\ell=1}^{L} z_\ell^j a_\ell^j V^j = py^j - r^j. \tag{1.13}$$

Equilibrium of firm j requires

$$\frac{py^j - r^j}{\Sigma_\ell a_\ell^j z_\ell^j} \geqslant \frac{p\bar{y}^j - r^j}{\Sigma_\ell a_\ell^j \bar{z}_\ell^j} \quad \text{for all } (\bar{y}^j, \bar{z}^j) \text{ in } Y^j. \tag{1.14}$$

The rent r^j imputed to firm j is redistributed among the consumers according to some fixed rule.

There is a set of consumers, indexed $i = 1, \ldots, I$. Each consumer i receives a share θ_{ij} of the rent r^j, $\theta_{ij} \geqslant 0$, $\Sigma_{i=1}^I \theta_{ij} = 1, j = 1, \ldots, J$. The share θ_{ij} may possibly reflect historical property rights, or it may reflect consumer i's marginal share in the budget of a state collecting all the rents (in which case $\theta_{ij} = \theta_i$ for all j).

Consumer i decides freely what firm or firms he or she belongs to, and what quantities of each type of labour he or she supplies there. (In conformity with standard general equilibrium theory, I am ignoring here the indivisibilities applicable to most jobs. I comment on that simplification in section 3.1.) Let then z_ℓ^{ij} denote the quantity of labour type ℓ performed by consumer i in firm j. The total labour income of consumer i is then $\Sigma_{\ell=1}^L \Sigma_{j=1}^J z_\ell^{ij} a_\ell^j V^j$. If consumer i initially holds quantities $(w_1^i, \ldots, w_g^i, \ldots, w_G^i) = w^i$ of the physical commodities, then his or her disposable income, say b^i, is defined as

$$b^i = pw^i + \Sigma_\ell \Sigma_j z_\ell^{ij} a_\ell^j V^j + \Sigma_j \theta_{ij} r^j. \tag{1.15}$$

This income is used by i to purchase consumer goods in quantities $(x_1^i, \ldots, x_G^i) = x^i$.

Recognising that i's income depends upon the prices p, the rents $(r^1, \ldots, r^J) = r$ and the labour weights $[a^j_\ell] = A$ (an $L \times J$ matrix), we may define as follows i's *budget set*:

$$B^i(p,r,A) = \{(x^i,z^i) \mid px^i \leqslant pw^i + \Sigma_\ell \Sigma_j z^{ij}_\ell a^j_\ell V^j + \Sigma_j \theta_{ij} r^j\}. \qquad (1.16)$$

It is assumed that i is able to consume vectors x^i and to perform quantities of labour $z^i = \Sigma_j z^{ij}$ belonging to a consumption set C^i in R^{G+L}, ordered by well-defined preferences $\succsim_i$. Equilibrium of consumer i requires

$$(x^i,z^i) \succsim_i (\bar{x}^i,\bar{z}^i) \quad \text{for all } (\bar{x}^i,\bar{z}^i) \text{ in } B^i(p,r,A) \cap C^i. \qquad (1.17)$$

That is, in equilibrium, all consumers choose freely their labour activities and their consumption so as to reach the highest utility level attainable under their budget constraint.

In the present formulation, consumer tastes are defined over vectors of labour activities and consumption, without regard for the firms where labour activities are carried out. This is restrictive, given people's concern for the human environment in which they work. A more general formulation is possible (see for example Drèze and Greenberg 1980) but less suitable for my purpose here.

An implication of the present formulation is that, at an equilibrium of consumer i, z^{ij}_ℓ cannot be positive unless $a^j_\ell V^j \geqslant a^k_\ell V^k$ for all $k = 1, \ldots, J$. Should there exist a firm k with $a^k_\ell V^k > a^j_\ell V^j$, then i would gain from reducing z^{ij}_ℓ to zero and increasing instead z^{ik}_ℓ, at no change in aggregate labour supply, but at a gain in disposable income.

We may bring all these elements together, and define a *labour-management equilibrium for a market economy* to consist of:

(i) A production plan (y^j,z^j) in Y^j for each firm j

(ii) A labour and consumption plan (x^i,z^i) in C^i, and a labour allocation matrix $Z^i = [z^{ij}_\ell]$ satisfying $z^i_\ell = \Sigma_j z^{ij}_\ell$, for each consumer i

(iii) A price vector p in R^G, a vector of rents r in R^J_+ (with $r^j = 0$ for all $j > K$), a matrix of labour weights $A = [a^j_\ell]$, such that the following conditions hold:

(iv) Feasibility for physical commodities:

$$\Sigma_i x^i \leqslant \Sigma_j y^j + \Sigma_i w^i \qquad (1.18)$$

(v) Feasibility for labour:

$$\text{for each } j, \quad \Sigma_i z^{ij} = z^j \qquad (1.19)$$

(vi) Maximization of value added per unit of labour:

$$\text{for each } j, \quad \frac{py^j - r^j}{\Sigma_\ell a^j_\ell z^j_\ell} \geqslant \frac{p\bar{y}^j - r^j}{\Sigma_\ell a^j_\ell \bar{z}^j_\ell} \quad \text{for all } (\bar{y}^j, z^j) \text{ in } Y^j \qquad (1.14)$$

(vii) Financial feasibility of consumer choices:

$$\text{for each } i, \quad (x^i, z^i) \text{ belongs to } B^i(p,r,A) \qquad (1.20)$$

(viii) Optimality of consumer choices:

$$\text{for each } i, \quad (x^i, z^i) \succsim_i (\bar{x}^i, \bar{z}^i) \quad \text{for all } (\bar{x}^i, \bar{z}^i) \text{ in } B^i(p,r,A) \cap C^i. \qquad (1.17)$$

Contrast with competitive equilibria

This definition looks perhaps forbidding. A closer look reveals that it follows closely the standard definition of a competitive equilibrium.[9] Indeed, the physical stipulations (i), (ii), (iv) and (v) must hold under any institutional arrangements. What is specific to labour management is the decision rules of firms, and the way in which information about labour opportunities is transmitted to consumers. In contrast, a *competitive equilibrium for a private ownership economy* consists of (i), (ii) and

(iii)′ A price vector p in R^G and a vector of wages and salaries s in R^L, such that conditions (iv) and (v) hold; as well as

(vi)′ Profit maximization:

$$\text{for each } j, \quad py^j - sz^j \geqslant p\bar{y}^j - s\bar{z}^j \quad \text{for all } (\bar{y}^j, \bar{z}^j) \text{ in } Y^j \qquad (1.21)$$

and (vii) and (viii), with the budget set of consumer i now defined as

$$B^i(p,s) = \{(x^i, z^i) \mid px^i \leqslant pw^i + sz^i + \Sigma_j \theta_{ij}(py^j - sz^j)\}. \qquad (1.22)$$

The differences between the two concepts thus concern the decision rule for business firms and the rules for income formation of the consumers. On the first score, maximization of value added per hour worked has replaced maximization of profit, net of labour costs but gross of capital rents. On the second score, shares in value added and in rents have replaced salaries and shares in profits. But the general structure of the two concepts is analogous, reflecting physical feasibility in (i), (ii), (iv) and (v), financial feasibility in (vii), decentralization of information in (iii), and optimality of individual decisions (given the information signals) in (vi) and (viii).

Both definitions achieve complete separation of the production and consumption decisions, and overall compatibility of the decentralized individual decisions. Both definitions characterize abstract 'equilibrium' situations of a kind never fully observed in reality. Thus all agents accept the information signals (prices, rents, income shares or alternatively wages and salaries) and do not recognize any influence of their own decisions on those parameters. In particular, any form of monopolistic behaviour is excluded. Also, every market clears exactly. In the case of labour, this means that nobody would strictly prefer to fill a job held by someone else – a point to which I return in section 1.5.

Why should one be interested in equilibrium concepts which overlook all these imperfections, hardly avoidable in realistic situations? One answer is that abstract theoretical models, where these imperfections are ignored, are useful to check the general consistency of a form of economic organization. The test of consistency typically takes the form of an existence theorem: under explicit assumptions about the primitive (extra-economic) data, an equilibrium is shown to exist; it is thus a logical possibility, free of internal contradiction. If the test were not passed, one would feel inhibited in discussing properties of a form of organization, which might not have been consistently defined.

As against this merit must always be weighed the danger of oversimplification. It could be that realistic imperfections are so severe as to deprive an equilibrium concept of any relevance. Reliance on the concept could then be misleading and positively harmful. Our present topic illustrates both points, reminding us that an existence theorem provides a necessary, but not a sufficient, condition for an equilibrium concept to be worthy of interest.

An equivalence property

To continue with the positive side, I may mention that my own interest in defining formally a general equilibrium concept for the labour-managed market economy arose from objections raised against the possibility of reconciling that form of organization with the requirements of economic efficiency. Would a labour-managed firm adopt the economically most efficient technology? In particular, would it foster labour-saving technological progress? Would it make efficient use of specialized skills, and provide adequate incentives for the acquisition of such skills?

A clear-cut answer to all these questions is provided by theorems A.3 and A.4 in appendix 1. These propositions formalize the conclusions presented in chapter 7 of Vanek (1970). They are summarized in a concise corollary.

Corollary 1.1

Under a minimal assumption,[10] the sets of allocations that can be sustained as competitive equilibria and as labour-management equilibria are identical.

This useful result is proved as follows. First, the physical allocation corresponding to any labour-management equilibrium can be sustained as a competitive equilibrium (theorem A.3). The prices p of physical commodities remain unchanged. The wages and salaries s are defined as follows:

$$s_\ell = \max_j a_\ell^j V^j \qquad \ell = 1, \ldots, L. \tag{1.23}$$

That is, wages correspond to the highest income shares which the different labour types command at the labour-management equilibrium; as already noted, condition (viii) in the definition implies that no labour of type ℓ is used in a firm k where $a_\ell^k V^k$ would fall short of this s_ℓ. The proof then consists in showing that, for all j, (y^j, z^j) actually maximizes profits $py - sz$ on Y^j, with $py^j - sz^j = r^j$; that is, with profits at the competitive equilibrium equal to the imputed rents at the labour-management equilibrium. A given matrix $\Theta = [\theta_{ij}]$ then leads to identical budget sets, and hence to identical choices, for all consumers. This completes the first part of the proof.

Second, the physical allocation corresponding to any competitive equilibrium can be sustained as a labour-management equilibrium (theorem A.4). Again, the prices of physical commodities remain unchanged, and the imputed rents are set equal to the competitive profits. The proof then consists in showing the existence of a matrix of labour weights $A = [a_\ell^j]$ such that

$$a_\ell^j \frac{py^j - r^j}{\Sigma_\ell a_\ell^j z_\ell^j} \leqslant s_\ell \qquad j = 1, \ldots, J \qquad \ell = 1, \ldots, L, \tag{1.24}$$

with equality whenever $z_\ell^j > 0$; and such that (y^j, z^j) actually maximizes on Y^j the value added per unit of labour V^j corresponding to these weights.

The plausibility of these results flows directly from formula (1.11), revealing that (in the differentiable case) shares in value added would reflect the marginal value products of all labour types. At a competitive equilibrium, marginal value products are equated to wages rates. Corollary 1.1 may be interpreted as stating that labour mobility between labour-managed firms entails the same equilibrium properties as competitive labour markets. In other words, the choices of the labour weights $[a_\ell^j]$, which determine incomes and labour inputs in labour-managed firms, are compatible with equilibrium only if they reflect the market clearing wages of a hypothetical associated competitive economy.

Comments

This conclusion is at the same time sobering and gratifying. (Many among my students regard it as an anticlimax.) It is definitely gratifying, in that it establishes the internal consistency of the labour-management equilibrium concept, under the same assumptions which guarantee the internal consistency of the Walrasian equilibrium concept. As a by-product, we know that a labour-management equilibrium (at which no consumer is satiated) is Pareto optimal. And we can rely on the well-developed theory of competitive economies to handle questions of existence, uniqueness, continuity, stability and so on for equilibria in labour-managed market economies.

A most gratifying aspect is that we have established unequivocally the compatibility of labour management with economic efficiency. More specifically, any Pareto-optimal allocation can be sustained as a labour-management equilibrium, under standard assumptions, through a conformable reallocation of the initial resources w^i and property rights or tax liabilities $[\theta_{ij}]$. Of course the standard assumptions are restrictive, in particular on the production side, where they exclude increasing returns to scale. It would have been unreasonable to expect a free lunch there!

To repeat, we have established precisely that economic efficiency is not a ground for objection to self-management, in the abstract context where competitive capitalism is efficient (complete markets, non-increasing returns and so on). This result is valuable, given the first ground on which economists are interested in labour management. Less obviously perhaps, but equally importantly, the result bears on our second ground of interest, and on a running theme of this book. Labour management is, in theory, compatible with other forms of economic organization, as long as equilibrium is attained. Thus labour-managed and capitalist firms could coexist, with consumers supplying their labour to both on equal terms, and with both types of firm trading physical commodities on the same markets. What is more, labour-managed shops could exist within capitalist firms, and some salaried labour could be employed by labour-managed firms. As long as the supply and demand for each type of labour in each firm are equal, overall consistency is maintained. Conversely, departures of prevailing economic decisions from those which might emerge under labour management can be identified as departures from a competitive equilibrium.

These implications are definitely useful. They may be combined with the similar results reached by Lange (1938) in *On the Economic Theory of Socialism*, to draw the broader conclusion that economic efficiency is in principle compatible with alternative institutional frameworks, at this level of abstraction.

The sobering side is that a generalization of labour management might fail to eradicate the inequalities in the distribution of income which are witnessed in most existing economies. Indeed, shares in value added would still reflect marginal value products, and rents charged to labour-managed firms would correspond to competitive profits. This point deserves special attention; it is taken up in section 1.5.

1.4 Information requirements and capital rents

An important difference between the two equilibrium concepts reviewed in section 1.3 is the nature of information signals on which decentralized individual decisions are based.

Both concepts have one signal in common, namely the prices p of physical commodities. In general equilibrium theory, commodities are dated, so that interest rates are implicit in the definition of prices. Thus all firms (whether capitalist or labour managed) pay interest charges on the financial capital needed for their production activities.

The additional signal used in defining a competitive equilibrium is the vector s of wages and salaries. Profits, in the firms $j = 1, \ldots, K$ where returns to scale need not be constant, are in the nature of residuals.[11] However, these profits appear in the budget constraints of the consumers, where they account for the property incomes $\Sigma_j \theta_{ij}(py^j - sz^j)$. Hence, information about profits must be transmitted to consumers; or else all consumers must hold correct expectations about property incomes. In the more realistic applications of general equilibrium theory, this aspect sometimes raises a modelling difficulty; see for instance the comments in Malinvaud (1977) or Drèze (1985c).

Under labour management, the additional signals are the rents imputed on pre-existing production facilities and the incomes $a_\ell^j V^j$ accruing to the different types of labour in the various firms. In equilibrium, the rents are equal to the corresponding competitive profits – but they are not 'residuals'. On the contrary, they influence the production decisions. This is readily seen in the differentiable example in section 1.2, with a single type of labour. Equilibrium of the firm was given by equation (1.8), which may be rewritten as

$$zp\frac{dy}{dz} - py + r = 0 \qquad (1.8)'$$

implying (by total differentiation)

$$\frac{\mathrm{d}z}{\mathrm{d}r} = \frac{-1}{zp\,\mathrm{d}^2y/\mathrm{d}z^2} > 0 \qquad \frac{\mathrm{d}V}{\mathrm{d}r} = -\frac{1}{z} < 0. \qquad (1.25)$$

Thus if the rent level is set too low, the employment level will be lower, and the value added per unit of labour will be higher, than with the correct rent level. An indication of an incorrect rent level will thus be provided by a comparision of labour incomes in the firm with outside alternatives. If the rent is too low, incomes will be higher, and outside workers will queue up to join the firm; equilibrium is not attained. If the rent is too high, attainable incomes will be lower, and no group of workers will care to operate the firm, if they have opportunities elsewhere.

We thus see that equilibrium of the labour supply by consumers automatically implies equilibrium levels for the capital rents. This could in principle make the system operational. To the best of my knowledge, however, its dynamics have not been studied. Would, for instance, a *tâtonnement* process in the prices of physical commodities, the labour weights $[a_\ell^j]$ and the rent levels r^j, converge under the same (admittedly restrictive) conditions under which a similar Walrasian process in (p,s) converges? The question deserves investigation.

In considering dynamic adjustments, proper attention should be paid to incentives. If rent levels are automatically raised when value added per worker rises above its level elsewhere, there will be no incentives for members of the firm to seek productivity gains. Conversely, higher incomes may reflect higher labour productivity rather than an insufficient rent level.

On the other hand, adjustments in rent levels as market data change play an important role in short-run dynamics. As already noted by the first authors in the field (see Ward 1958; Domar 1966; Vanek 1970) the first-order condition (1.8)′ implies that employment and production respond *negatively* to an increase in p, when r is kept fixed; that is, the supply function is backward sloping. Indeed, total differentiation of (1.8)′ yields

$$\frac{\mathrm{d}z}{\mathrm{d}p} = \frac{y - z\,\mathrm{d}y/\mathrm{d}z}{zp\,\mathrm{d}^2y/\mathrm{d}z^2} = \frac{r}{zp^2\,\mathrm{d}^2y/\mathrm{d}z^2} < 0. \tag{1.26}$$

If instead r is adjusted so as to keep value added per worker constant, as required by labour market equilibrium, then $\mathrm{d}r/\mathrm{d}p = y > 0$ and $\mathrm{d}z/\mathrm{d}p$ becomes

$$\left.\frac{\mathrm{d}z}{\mathrm{d}p}\right|_V = \frac{r}{zp^2\,\mathrm{d}^2y/\mathrm{d}z^2} - \frac{y}{zp\,\mathrm{d}^2y/\mathrm{d}z^2} = -\frac{\mathrm{d}y/\mathrm{d}z}{p\,\mathrm{d}^2y/\mathrm{d}z^2}$$
$$= \frac{-V}{p^2\,\mathrm{d}^2y/\mathrm{d}z^2} > 0. \tag{1.27}$$

The supply curve is now upward sloping.

We must accordingly conclude that proper adjustments in capital rents are essential to the attainment of a labour-management equilibrium. This requirement is apt to raise practical difficulties, as the Yugoslav experience suggests; see in particular Vanek and Jovicic (1975), Estrin (1981) or Estrin and Svejnar (1982). One must admit that adjustments in capital rents are a roundabout way of bringing the supply and demand for *labour* into equilibrium. Wage adjustments provide a more transparent device. Alternatively, wage policies provide a more transparent device than capital rents for arbitrating efficiency and equity aspects of non-clearing labour markets, as discussed in chapter 5.

In an economy with myriads of small firms, the adjustments in capital rents would be cumbersome to administer. Considerations of uncertainty with incomplete markets, as introduced in chapter 4, lead to specify state-dependent (stochastic) capital rents. I shall argue, with others, that the associated difficulties go a long way towards explaining the limited extension of labour management in modern industrial economies.

1.5 Income distribution

As noted at the end of section 1.3, a labour-management equilibrium entails a distribution of income where labour earnings reflect marginal value products, and rents corresponding to competitive profits are charged to labour-managed firms and redistributed as property income. This conclusion might be interpreted as ruling out equalitarian sharing rules of the kind practiced in kibbutzim, or semi-equalitarian rules with individual incomes ranging from 1 to 3 for instance. Such a conclusion would be somewhat hasty, because (as noted in section 1.2) the agreement of labour earnings and marginal value products is a mere consequence of efficient use of labour, and is *in itself* fully compatible with any degree of equality or inequality.[12]

I have already remarked that, in equilibrium, everyone would be satisfied with his or her job, given the prevailing earning structure, and would not strictly prefer the job(s) held by anyone else. These conditions are clearly violated in Western economies, due not only to unemployment but also to the fact that some firms pay higher wages than others for similar work (think about the high wages paid by central banks, by profit-making nationalized utilities, by high-profits firms or sectors); or to the fact that some well-compensated positions of authority for which several equally qualified applicants exist are filled on the basis of seniority, family or educational ties, political patronage and so on; or to the fact that people commute to perform at some distance work which also exists near their homes. All these cases violate the equilibrium condition of consumers in their labour supply.[13]

Before asking whether labour management would reduce or eliminate some of these imperfections, I wish to reflect first on the nature of the inequalities accepted by our equilibrium concepts. Clearly, equilibrium requires equal earnings for equal work, no matter where or by whom it is performed. And equilibrium allows for the remuneration of individual productivity differentials in carrying out standard tasks.[14] But what about the earnings associated with different types of labour? The main property of equilibrium is that labour type k could not entail higher earnings than labour type ℓ, if there exist workers engaged in type ℓ who could just as well perform type k, and would be prepared to do so without additional compensation. For instance, a desired position of authority for which there exist several qualified candidates could not entail an increase in earnings. But work on the night shift could entail higher earnings than work on the day shift, if a majority of workers prefer the day shift. (Note that this implies a form of rent for those workers who actually prefer working at night.)

It follows that, in equilibrium, lower earnings in labour type ℓ than in the equally or more attractive labour type k could only reflect an insufficient supply of type k workers – insufficient, that is, to increase employment in type k to the point where the two marginal value products are equalized. To illustrate the point, many firms would gladly use graduate engineers as fitters, or use weight-lifters to push wheelbarrows, if there were enough engineers and weight-lifters around. What stops them from actually doing so is the limited supply of engineers and weight-lifters, which results in the need to economize their skills, reserving them for jobs with high marginal value products and hence high earnings in equilibrium. Clearly, the road to greater equality goes through education and training – due account being taken of the cost of these activities in calculating the present values of lifetime incomes. It is not surprising that provisions for education and training are stressed in all forms of cooperatives, labour-managed firms, kibbutzim and so on.[15]

This being said, there remains the distinct possibility that major earnings differentials between occupations reflect artificial barriers to entry (to US medical schools?) and/or that professional incomes are used to sustain an allocation of individuals to jobs on the basis of criteria such as patronage, rather than to guide it efficiently in the first place: you are competent because you are well paid, and not the other way around!

Labour management could change this state of affairs in two ways: by bringing the allocation of labour closer to equilibrium, or by generating different equilibria where the allocation of labour is divorced from income differentials. The first way is a distinct possibility, but some aspects of the Yugoslav experience provide a ground for caution.[16]

The second way boils down to this. In a kibbutz, where members with very different skills work together and enjoy the same real income, one may presume that individual labour is used efficiently. Also, the moral standards of members make the system internally stable. What is there to prevent that system from being globally stable? This is a problem in the allocation of labour *between* kibbutzim, or between kibbutzim and other types of firms. What is required here is that nobody should leave a kibbutz unless it be to fill a job where his or her marginal value product exceeds, not his or her current income, but rather his or her current marginal value product. Conversely, a person should be prepared to leave in order to contribute more – due recognition being given to non-material aspects, like a person's contribution to and appreciation of the quality of life in a given environment. In other words, the allocation of labour should be guided by shadow prices instead of personal incomes. Is that possible? It is not in a capitalist organization, where employees draw a clear distinction between their own interests and those of their employer. The distinction is less obvious in the case of self-managed organizations – but the problem of allocating labour efficiently between firms is there.

This line of reasoning leads directly to a consideration of the rules governing the withdrawal of members from labour-managed organizations – a subject that will not be covered here.[17] Clearly, this type of overall organization goes well beyond the simple principles underlying the equilibrium concepts introduced in section 1.3.

Before leaving the subject, I should mention the obvious point that property incomes are governed by exogenous rules – the θ_{ij} – in both equilibrium concepts. In actual situations, these rules are apt to reflect the values of society as well as its historical past. One would expect labour-management systems to generate different values from those prevailing in systems less closely geared to democratic principles.

1.6 Working conditions

In concluding this chapter, I wish to say a few words about the choice of working conditions in a firm. My purpose is not to treat the subject extensively, but rather to introduce through a simple example a feature that will prove central in later chapters, namely aggregation of individual preferences.

So far, we have taken as given a list of L types of labour and we have let the firm choose the quantities of each type used as inputs. Although I have not been explicit on that point, my examples have suggested that types of labour might correspond to qualifications (bricklaying or accounting), work content (carrying logs or carrying teacups) or work schedules (day shift or night shift). But more qualitative aspects of the labour process, generally called 'working conditions', deserve consideration as well. Thus on an assembly line, the speed of the line, the nature of the work performed at each post and the design of the working posts themselves are relevant to both productivity and the comfort of workers. In many production processes, these characteristics of working conditions are not exogenous; they may be varied continuously, subject only to the constraint that a single choice be made, which applies simultaneously to all workers concerned. For this reason, the choice of characteristics is a public decision, comparable with the choice of production levels for public goods (like fire protection), of location for a single facility serving many consumers (like a bus stop), or of qualitative characteristics for a consumer good (like an automobile) purchased by many consumers.

The nature of the problem is well illustrated by the example introduced in section 1.2 of a firm using a single type of labour. Working conditions will be identified with a vector of characteristics $(b_1, \ldots, b_c, \ldots, b_C) = b$. The production set Y is now defined in the space of physical commodities y, quantity of labour z and labour characteristics b. As the characteristics b vary, the quantity of labour z required to produce a net output vector y may vary. This feature will be summarized by writing $y(z,b)$ for the vector of physical quantities which maximizes py over Y for given z *and* b. Thus, value added becomes $py(z,b) - r$ and value added per unit of labour becomes

$$V(z,b) = \frac{py(z,b) - r}{z}. \tag{1.28}$$

Working conditions also affect the well-being of workers, whose preferences are now defined in terms of income, quantity of labour and characteristics of labour. These preferences will be represented by individual utility functions $u^i(x^i,z^i,b) = u^i(z^iV,z^i,b)$.

If there was a single worker, he or she would choose simultaneously z and b to maximize $u(py(z,b) - r,z,b)$. The first-order conditions would be:

$$\frac{du}{dz} = \frac{\partial u}{\partial x} p \frac{\partial y}{\partial z} + \frac{\partial u}{\partial z} = 0$$

$$\frac{du}{db_c} = \frac{\partial u}{\partial x} p \frac{\partial y}{\partial b_c} + \frac{\partial u}{\partial b_c} = 0 \qquad c = 1, \ldots, C \tag{1.29}$$

$$\left.\frac{dz}{db_c}\right|_u = \left.\frac{dz}{db_c}\right|_y \qquad p\frac{\partial y}{\partial b_c} = \left.\frac{dx}{db_c}\right|_u . \tag{1.30}$$

Condition (1.30) states that the marginal rate of substitution (utility-wise) between working time z and working characteristic b_c is equal to their marginal rate of transformation (production-wise). Alternatively, the marginal value product of characteristic b_c is equal to the marginal rate of substitution (utility-wise) between that characteristic and disposable income, sometimes called 'marginal willingness to pay for characteristic b_c'.

With several workers, choice of working conditions becomes a group decision, involving aggregation of individual preferences. The weakest criterion for efficient group decisions is that of Pareto optimality. Application of that criterion leads to the following maximization problem, with undetermined weights λ^i:

$$\max_b \sum_i \lambda^i u^i \left(z^i \frac{py(z,b) - r}{z}, z^i, b \right). \tag{1.31}$$

The first-order conditions are:

$$\sum_i \lambda^i \left(\frac{\partial u^i}{\partial x^i} \frac{z^i p}{z} \frac{\partial y}{\partial b_c} + \frac{\partial u^i}{\partial b_c} \right) = 0 \qquad c = 1, \ldots, C \tag{1.32}$$

$$p\frac{\partial y}{\partial b_c} = \left(\sum_i \lambda^i \frac{\partial u^i}{\partial x^i} \left.\frac{dx^i}{db_c}\right|_{u^i} \right) \Big/ \left(\sum_i \lambda^i \frac{\partial u^i}{\partial x^i} \frac{z^i}{z} \right)$$

$$\frac{\partial V}{\partial b_c} = \left(\sum_i \lambda^i \frac{\partial u^i}{\partial x^i} z^i \left.\frac{dV}{db_c}\right|_{u^i} \right) \Big/ \left(\sum_i \lambda^i \frac{\partial u^i}{\partial x^i} z^i \right). \tag{1.33}$$

Conditions (1.33) state that the marginal value product of each characteristic b_c, $p\,\partial y/\partial b_c$, is equal to a weighted sum of the individual marginal willingnesses to pay for that characteristic, $dx^i/db_c|_{u^i}$, where the weights are the *same* for each characteristic. (Alternatively, these conditions are expressed in terms of the impact of each characteristic on value added per hour worked, in which case the weights add up to unity.)

One may look at $\lambda^i \partial u^i/\partial x^i$ as a measure of the weight assigned by the firm to the income of member i. If these weights were all equal, then (1.33) would reduce to

$$p\frac{\partial y}{\partial b_c} = \sum_i \frac{\mathrm{d}x^i}{\mathrm{d}b_c}\bigg|_{u^i} \qquad c = 1, \ldots, C. \tag{1.34}$$

This formula is analogous to the Lindahl-Samuelson conditions for efficient provision of public goods, when lump-sum transfers of income or personalized prices are available to bring about equality of the terms $\lambda^i \partial u^i/\partial x^i$, or when no further transfers are deemed desirable at the prevailing income distribution.

As a simple application of this analysis, I consider by way of conclusion the case of a single characteristic, namely working hours in a firm where technological requirements impose identical working hours for all members (as might be the case for an assembly line, a distant construction site or a fishing boat). Writing ℓ for working hours, and recognizing that V is independent of ℓ when the number of members is freely adjusted, problem (1.31) reduces to

$$\max_{\ell} \sum_i \lambda^i u^i(\ell V, \ell). \tag{1.35}$$

The first-order condition is simply

$$\sum_i \lambda^i \left(\frac{\partial u^i}{\partial x^i} V + \frac{\partial u^i}{\partial z^i}\right) = 0$$

$$V = \left(\sum_i \lambda^i \frac{\partial u^i}{\partial x^i} \frac{\mathrm{d}x^i}{\mathrm{d}z^i}\bigg|_{u^i}\right) \bigg/ \left(\sum_i \lambda^i \frac{\partial u^i}{\partial x^i}\right) \tag{1.36}$$

and reduces to

$$V = \sum_i \frac{\mathrm{d}x^i}{\mathrm{d}z^i}\bigg|_{u^i} \tag{1.37}$$

when the weights $\lambda^i \partial u^i/\partial x^i$ are equal.

The term $\mathrm{d}x^i/\mathrm{d}z^i|_{u^i}$ is often called the 'reservation wage' of member i. Condition (1.36) states that value added per hour worked should be equated to a weighted average of the reservation wages of the members – or a simple arithmetic average in the case of equal weights. If the individual reservation wages were symmetrically distributed over the members, their arithmetic average would be equal to their median, and condition (1.36) could be implemented through a voting procedure.

Notes

1 A streamlined version of this chapter, originally developed in Drèze (1974c) and briefly summarized in sections 2 and 3 of Drèze (1976), is available in French in Drèze (1984) and translated into English as Drèze (1985a).

2 For a reasonably up-to-date bibliography, see Bartlett and Uvalic (1985).

3 Also, a few papers consider bargaining between workers and management: see for instance Steinherr (1977) or Svejnar (1982).

4 The framework includes as a logical possibility an application to situations of uncertainty with a full set of insurance markets, that is with an insurance market for each commodity contingent on each possible state of the environment. No reference to that application will be made in this chapter.

5 Indeed, for all λ in (0,1), the point $[\lambda y(z_1) + (1-\lambda)y(z_2), \lambda z_1 + (1-\lambda)z_2]$ belongs to Y and $py[\lambda z_1 + (1-\lambda)z_2] \geqslant \lambda py(z_1) + (1-\lambda)py(z_2)$.

6 The determination of the level of the rent is discussed in sections 1.3 and 1.4. The word 'rent' is used here as a short form of 'capital rental price'.

7 Thus kibbutzim maintain *equality* in the distribution of real income, irrespective of contributions to labour inputs. At the time of the report by Oakeshott (1973), salaries at Mondragon ranged from 1 to 3 over all types of labour (including management), with a 5 per cent bonus for the night shifts.

8 Again, conditions (1.10) and (1.11) can be generalized to the non-differentiable case. Also second-order conditions can be specified – which need not detain us here.

9 At least, the definition which is standard in general equilibrium theory. There is another definition, found in many introductory textbooks, which runs in terms of conditions loosely identified as sufficient for the realization of a competitive equilibrium (like a large number of insignificant traders on both sides of each market, and so on).

10 See appendix 1: preferences should be monotone. Existence of either type of equilibrium naturally requires additional assumptions.

11 In firms $j = K + 1, \ldots, J$, competitive profits are equal to zero.

12 This section has been influenced by the work of my colleague Robert Leroy (1983) and by stimulating discussions with him.

13 The role of uncertainty in explaining some - not all - of these distortions is alluded to in chapter 2.

14 Again, uncertainty about individual abilities may justify risk-sharing schemes absorbing some of these differences.

15 On this point see for example Laakkonen (1977). Special reference should also be made to those cases where quality of performance is so highly valued as to create excessive demand for particular skills. Everybody would prefer to undergo surgery under the best conditions available, to watch artists of the highest quality, or to be taught elementary economics by Kenneth Arrow! In these cases inequality in the personal distribution of incomes tends to increase, as the rich express their demand for quality in financial terms. But these cases remain exceptional and are peripheral to my subject.

16 See the references given at the end of section 1.4.

17 Again, uncertainty introduces new considerations of relevance to this point. See also the comments by Meade (1972, section 5) and by Drèze and Greenberg (1980).

CHAPTER 2

Stock-market Economies

2.1 Introduction to chapters 2–4

Market failures

The static general equilibrium analysis reviewed in chapter 1 has obvious limitations. Referring specifically to the concept of competitive equilibrium, one may organize these limitations under three headings, corresponding to three logically distinct departures from the idealized condition that each market is cleared (physically) at prices to which all agents adjust, accepting them as exogenous data. The three cases are: (i) many markets do not exist at all; (ii) some markets do not clear, and either demand or more typically supply is subject to non-price rationing (unemployment and unused capacity being the foremost examples); (iii) some markets clear at non-competitive prices (due, for instance, to monopolistic behaviour by suppliers).

Some literature has been devoted to a comparison of monopolistic pressures in capitalist and labour-managed economies; see in particular Vanek (1970, chapter 16), Meade (1972, section 2.4; 1974) or Steinherr and Vanek (1976). That literature will not be reviewed here.

Non-clearing labour markets are discussed in section 5.3. Incomplete markets, with specific reference to insurance markets or other markets designed to cope with uncertainty, are the subject of this chapter, of the next chapter (for the case of capitalist firms drawing labour contracts) and of sections 4.1 and 4.2 (for the case of labour-managed firms).

Uncertainty, states of the environment and insurance values

The theory in chapter 1 was presented for a world of certainty. At the general equilibrium level, we took as known and given an *environment* consisting of initial resources, consumer preferences and a technology. In reality, the environment is not given, but depends upon uncertain events.[1] It would thus be more natural to take as a starting-point a set of possible (mutually exclusive) *states of the environment*, or states of the world in a widely used terminology. Given a complete list of alternative states, the conceptual model can be extended by the introduction of a full set of insurance markets, covering all possible contingencies.[2]

Under that extension, the definition of a competitive equilibrium includes a set of *plans*, one for each consumer specifying his consumption and labour supply under every possible contingency, and one for each firm specifying its inputs and outputs under every possible contingency. It also includes a set of *insurance prices*, one for each commodity or labour service contingent on every possible state, in terms of which consumption and production plans have a unique well-defined insurance value. Firms maximize the insurance value of their production plan, over a production set defined in the space of contingent commodities. And consumers maximize the expected utility of their consumption plan under a single budget constraint expressed in terms of insurance value.[3]

The insurance markets serve *two* functions in that model. They enable consumers to reallocate their resources across alternative states of the environment; this is a risk-sharing function, typically associated with insurance. They provide to consumers and especially to producers information about the economic evaluation of risks, thereby guiding efficient decisions (about occupational choices, investments and so on).[4]

Although presented for a world of certainty, the theory of chapter 1 applies as well to a world of uncertainty with a complete set of insurance markets. In particular, the notion of value added per unit of labour remains well defined, with 'value' now understood as 'insurance value'. Labour-management equilibria are thus also well defined, and so are competitive equilibria; the identity relation between the two sets of equilibria is preserved, and no new theoretical issues arise.

Asset markets and investment decisions

In capitalist economies, insurance markets are well developed for some risks, but conspicuously absent for other risks. Thus an independent practitioner can insure against his death or sickness, he can cover his professional liability, but he cannot insure against professional failure. A household can insure its house against fire or flood damages, but typically not against loss of economic value. Similarly, a firm can insure its plant against fire, but not against lack of profitability. Insurance of major recreational events against bad weather is now commonplace, but I have not heard of insurance contracts covering independent research activities. The reduction to certainty through insurance is thus severely limited, and various authors have sought to explain this 'market failure' through moral hazards, adverse selection, transaction or computation costs, and so on.[5]

In capitalist economies, a partial substitute for missing insurance markets is found in asset markets, especially financial markets.[6] A stock exchange permits spreading business risks among a large number of individual shareholders, and stock prices provide an economic evaluation of business ventures. The economic theory of finance is concerned with the extent to which financial markets provide adequate opportunities for sharing efficiently the risks originating in our uncertain environment, and with the extent to which asset prices provide adequate information for guiding business decisions.

If there existed as many assets, with linearly independent returns, as there are possible states of the environment, then asset prices would reveal implicit insurance prices for all contingencies. Risk-sharing opportunities would be complete, and all economic projects would have a well-defined insurance value. This hypothetical situation is called 'complete spanning' in the theory of finance. In reality, spanning is incomplete; consumers cannot shed all the risks which they face, and business firms make investment decisions without finding in market prices a precise valuation of their uncertain future returns.

Consequently, the risk-sharing aspect becomes linked with the evaluation aspect. Because individuals differ in their ability and willingness to bear risks, efficient sharing requires that risks be ultimately borne by those individuals, or groups of individuals, best able to bear them. (Hopefully, individual portfolio choices, decentralized through a competitive stock market, may have that efficiency property.) The evaluation of investment projects will then reflect the attitudes towards specific risks of those individuals who bear them. More precisely, business decisions will be guided by the risk preferences of shareholders (holding efficient portfolios).

In the absence of complete spanning, shareholders will typically not be in full agreement about the evaluation of projects. Aggregation of their preferences is needed, and the theory of the firm becomes a theory of group decisions under uncertainty. Some implications of Pareto efficiency for these decisions have been studied.[7] On the positive side, there is no single generally accepted model of business decisions under uncertainty, but the nature of alternative approaches is by now well understood (see for example Drèze 1982).

A general equilibrium concept, extending early work by Diamond (1967), has been introduced in Drèze (1974b) and taken up in Grossman and Hart (1979); see also Gevers (1974). It combines competitive equilibrium on the stock market with production plans, in each firm, which are Pareto efficient from the viewpoint of that firm's shareholders. This concept, called 'stockholders equilibrium' by Drèze (1974b) and 'equilibrium of production and exchange' by Grossman and Hart (1979), is reviewed in section 2.2.

The Pareto-efficiency property is useful for the comparative purposes of chapter 4. For the purposes of positive analysis, a new approach is presented here which is both more general and more realistic. It aims at formalizing the organization of modern corporations: ultimate authority remains vested with shareholders, reaching majority decisions at general assemblies, but boards of directors exercise effective control and receive substantial discretion, which is partly delegated to managers. The 'control principle' of section 2.2 defines a selection from the Pareto-efficient set, on the basis of majority voting by shareholders, with veto rights for directors. (Extensions to multistage control and delegation are also outlined in section 2.2.)

Income uncertainty and labour contracts

The models of the theory of finance concentrate on the investment decisions of business firms and the efficient sharing among consumers and property owners of the risks embodied in physical capital. Yet, for most consumers, the major source of income is not assets but labour;

and the major source of uncertainty originates not in physical capital but in human capital. This is particularly true in periods of high unemployment. But even otherwise real wages and salaries are subject to significant deviations from trend; the demand for specific skills is apt to vary, especially at a particular firm or location; a person's productive abilities reveal themselves only progressively; promotion prospects typically entail selection; and incomes from independent practice are by nature uncertain. Insurance opportunities are almost non-existent for labour incomes, and diversification of human capital is severely restricted. As noted by Meade (1972): 'While property owners can spread their risks by putting small bits of their property into a large number of concerns, a worker cannot put small bits of his effort into a large number of different jobs.'[8]

In capitalist economies, a partial substitute for missing insurance markets covering human capital is found in labour contracts, which embody an element of risk-sharing between firms (shareholders) and their employees. If wages were adjusted continuously to reflect the marginal value product of labour at full employment, the incomes of workers might undergo intolerable fluctuations. Long-term labour contracts, stipulating the same employment levels but more stable wage levels, are more attractive to workers. Given a lesser degree of risk aversion on the part of shareholders (thanks to asset diversification), such contracts can be drawn on mutually advantageous terms. A stable wage, set somewhat below the expected value of the marginal value product of labour, will appeal to the risk-averse workers while raising expected profits sufficiently to compensate shareholders for the additional variability of profits.

This simple idea is translated, in the literature on (implicit) labour contracts, into properties of the profiles, across states, of employment and wage levels that are Pareto efficient from the viewpoint of the shareholders and workers in a given firm.[9] There is an interesting parallelism between the theory of labour contracts and that of stockholders equilibria. In such work as Holmström (1983), a competitive equilibrium on the market for labour contracts is combined with decisions in all firms (about employment and wage levels) which are Pareto efficient from the viewpoint of their members (shareholders and workers). The (Nash-Pareto) nature of that equilibrium concept is the same as in 'equilibria of production and exchange'. That parallelism has not been stressed in the literature, partly because it was obscured by special assumptions (like risk neutrality of shareholders), but mostly because the motivations were different (explaining downward wage rigidities and involuntary layoffs). It is brought out explicitly in chapter 3 in the concept of equilibrium of production and exchange with labour contracts, which integrates the two approaches. That concept combines equilibrium on the stock exchange and on the markets for labour contracts with two properties at the firm level: (i) the terms of the labour contract are Pareto efficient for the shareholders and workers, and no alternative terms would be simultaneously preferred by the directors, by a majority of shareholders and by a majority of workers; (ii) given the terms of the contract, production and employment are optimal from the viewpoint of the firm (of its directors and shareholders).

Integrating the theories of finance and of labour contracts

The integration of the theory of finance with that of labour contracts has substantive as well as formal relevance. Indeed, the two branches of economic theory are concerned with different aspects of a firm's policy. The theory of finance deals with investment decisions, which modify the production possibilities in the various states of the world. The theory of labour contracts deals with decisions about employment (hence output) in alternative states, and the division of the resulting gross value added between labour (wages) and capital (profits). Clearly, these aspects are interdependent. In particular, investment decisions affect the employment opportunities in the different states, whereas profits net of wages affect the attractiveness of investment.

This interdependence has not received the attention which it deserves.[10] And yet its existence has been confirmed in repeated empirical situations, and its source – embodied human capital – has been widely recognized in the literature.[11]

A firm is primarily an association of persons engaged together in production. Typically, the association uses some equipment, and accumulates know-how in operating it. Uncertainties about the future activities of the firm are uncertainties about the economic usefulness of the entire association; they affect simultaneously the human capital and the physical capital set to work in the firm.

The risk borne by each component of the firm depends upon several factors, in particular: the difference between its productivity (earning ability) inside and outside the firm; its mobility, either real or contractual; and the nature of risk-sharing agreements within the firm. Thus, a worker with highly specialized scarce skills valuable to a single firm may be well paid, on account of his high marginal productivity there, in spite of a low opportunity cost (the wages of an unskilled worker elsewhere). His vested interest in the continuation of the firm is substantial. If the firm contemplates a change of activity with high risk of failure, he may voice a strong opposition, especially if he is risk averse. In contrast, an equally well-paid worker whose skills are not specialized, so that he could earn the same wage elsewhere, may show little concern. Such will be the case provided this second worker's mobility is not otherwise constrained, for instance by the fact that alternative employment is only available at some other location, to which the worker does not care to move. In the case of physical equipment, use is apt to be quite specialized, and mobility rather restricted.[12] Financial capital is by definition non-specialized, although returns within the firm may be different from elsewhere, mobility may be restricted by contractual stipulations, and bankruptcy typically entails high transaction costs.

These problems must be considered in the light of risk-sharing agreements. Thus the worker with firm-specific skills could be convinced to accept the firm's change of activity, upon being promised adequate compensation (for the loss of his embodied human capital) in case of failure. The point which I want to stress is that his viewpoint should be recognized, and the compensation should be stipulated and possibly set aside, before the change is decided. Investment decisions and labour contracts are interrelated decisions, to be made jointly in the presence of embodied (firm-specific) human capital. The model, and the equilibrium concept, introduced in chapter 3 make a modest step in that direction. The step is modest because the model is simplified. (In particular, the two-period structure with all decisions reached in period 0 ignores important dynamic aspects, the relevance of which is illustrated in chapter 5.) Section 3.4 discusses some properties of Pareto-efficient labour contracts in a stock-market economy. An important aspect of that discussion is the characterization of efficient risk-sharing between property owners and workers, bringing together the contributions of labour contract theory and asset pricing theory, in terms used again in chapter 5 for the discussion of wage formation at the macroeconomic level. Although that discussion is still exploratory, it is an inspiring step in the direction of spelling out the macroeconomic implications of microeconomics[13] in an incomplete markets framework.

Capitalist firms versus labour-managed firms

The foregoing comments set the stage for contrasting (in chapter 4) capitalism and labour management, in a world of uncertainty with incomplete insurance markets. A capitalist firm is owned by shareholders, and supposedly managed in their interest; it hires labour, and draws contracts specifying wages and employment in alternative states; value added net of the wage bill (but gross of capital costs) defines residual profits; shareholders are concerned about state distributions of profits, and investment decisions should be guided by their (aggregated) preferences over such distributions. Exchange of shares on the stock market enables shareholders to diversify their risks. The labour contracts are assumed to be Pareto efficient from the viewpoint of the members of the firm (workers and shareholders), and compatible with equilibrium on the labour markets.

A labour-managed firm is organized by workers. In order to produce, the firm needs to invest and hence to raise (physical and/or) financial capital. It would seem unduly restrictive to stipulate that the financial capital is supplied entirely by the workers themselves; access to outside funds is bound to be needed, and hopefully may be forthcoming. A financial contract is then drawn between the workers and the suppliers of capital. To retain full generality, say that the contract stipulates an amount of repayment for each state (possibly, but not necessarily, an identical amount under all states). The workers then decide how to invest their capital and how much labour to supply under each state. After producing and repaying the stipulated amount, they are left with a (state-dependent) residual value added – net of capital costs but gross of labour costs. That value added is shared by the workers in accordance with some rule. For general equilibrium purposes, this picture needs to be completed with a definition of the equilibrium conditions for the supply and demand of both capital and labour.

Three remarks should be made about this presentation. First, the repayments for outside capital are a natural extension of the rents r (or r^j) considered in chapter 1.[14] The repayments and the rents alike may be viewed as a price paid for access to capital. Under uncertainty, it is only natural to stipulate a price under each state, leaving open at this stage the question whether or not the repayments should be allowed to vary with the state. (It should be clear at once that identical repayments correspond to financing by means of default-free bonds.)

Second, there is almost complete symmetry between the description here of a *modus operandi* for the capitalist firm and for the labour-managed firm. The labour contracts of the capitalist firm have as a counterpart the financial contracts of the labour-managed firm. The residual profits of the capitalist shareholders have as a counterpart the residual value added of the self-managed workers.[15] And we shall see below that the analogy can be pushed even further.

Third, the assumption that the labour contracts (which stipulate employment and wages under each state) are Pareto efficient for the members of the capitalist firms has a natural analogue in the labour-managed firms, namely that the financial contracts (which stipulate repayments under each state) are Pareto efficient for the members of the firm and the suppliers of capital.

Preview

These remarks suggest that an equivalence property, comparable with that stated in section 1.3, may also hold under uncertainty with incomplete markets. Such is indeed the case, as we shall verify in chapter 4: the sets of allocations that can be sustained as labour-management equilibria with Pareto-efficient equity contracts, and as equilibria of production and exchange with Pareto-efficient labour contracts, are equivalent. But an important caveat should be stressed, which has no counterpart in the 'complete markets' model of chapter 1. The equivalence is predicated on the *assumption* that both capitalist and labour-managed firms are able to generate Pareto-efficient contracts between their members, the suppliers of labour and capital. How the Pareto-efficient contracts are drawn remains to be discussed; that is clearly an important and largely unresolved issue. In contrast, the equivalence property of chapter 1 was obtained under well-defined decision rules for the firms: maximization of either profits or value added per unit of labour. In order to interpret the conclusions reached here, we shall need to evaluate more closely the prospects for Pareto-efficient contracting under the two systems (compare section 4.2). Chapter 4 will also consider the more realistic case where the contracts are not Pareto efficient.

Prior to that, I shall introduce the simple model of a stock-market economy in this chapter. I shall then define stockholders equilibria with labour contracts in chapter 3, where some properties of that concept are also discussed, and Pareto-efficient contracts are characterized.

2.2 Stockholders equilibria

The physical model

It will facilitate understanding if I review first the basic model of the theory of finance,[16] which is a very special case of the general model introduced in section 1.3.[17] There is a single physical commodity, and no labour. There are two periods, labelled 0 and 1, and S possible states of the environment, labelled $s = 1, \ldots, S$. The true state is unknown in period 0, but will be known in period 1.

A production plan for firm j is a vector y^j in R^{S+1}, where $y^j = (y^j_0, y^j_1, \ldots, y^j_S)$. Here $y^j_0 \leqslant 0$ is a level of investment in period 0, and $y^j_s \geqslant 0$ is a level of output in period 1 under state s. It is also convenient to denote by $y = (y^1, \ldots, y^J)$ in $R^{J(S+1)}$ a vector of production plans, one for each firm.

The production possibilities of firm j are fully described by its production set Y^j in R^{S+1}, the set of feasible production plans. This set describes how future outputs are related to current investment, and what opportunities are open to the firm for choosing a state distribution of outputs. A simple example goes as follows. A tomato farmer has the choice of two production techniques: outdoor production and greenhouse production. He contemplates two possible states of the environment, rainfall (r) or sunshine (s). Outdoor production yields a greater output (from a given investment) in state s than in state r, whereas greenhouse production yields the same output under both states. The production set Y stipulates what state distributions of outputs are obtained from given investments in either technique, or a combination of both. Under diminishing returns to scale in each technique, the production set Y in R^3 is strictly convex, and its projection in R^2 for given initial investment is also strictly convex.[18] (The reader is invited to consider any firm, whose 'outdoor' technique corresponds to physical investment and whose 'greenhouse' option corresponds to keeping money in the bank. Under state s, demand is 'sustained'; under state r it is 'reduced'.)

A consumption plan for consumer i is a vector x^i in R_+^{S+1}, where $x^i = (x_0^i, x_1^i, \ldots, x_S^i)$ defines consumption levels in period 0, and in period 1 under every possible state. The consumption set of i is still denoted $C^i \subset R_+^{S+1}$, and is ordered by the preference relation $\succsim_i$. This relation defines implicitly time preference, risk preference and subjective beliefs regarding the likelihood of the different states. Under the natural assumptions that preferences are additive with respect to the mutually exclusive states ('sure thing principle') and representable by a utility function (continuity), we may write

$$u^i(x^i) = \sum_{s=1}^{S} u_s^i(x_0^i, x_s^i). \tag{2.1}$$

If in addition the subjective beliefs of i regarding the likelihood of the states are represented by a probability vector ϕ^i, then we obtain the standard 'state-dependent' utility representation

$$u^i(x^i) = \sum_{s=1}^{S} \phi_s^i u_s^i(x_0^i, x_s^i). \tag{2.2}$$

Let as before $w^i = (w_0^i, w_1^i, \ldots, w_S^i)$ denote the initial endowment of consumer i (in period 0 and in period 1 under every state). A *physically feasible allocation* for this economy consists of a set of J production plans $y^j \in Y^j$ and I consumption plans $x^i \in C^i$ such that:

$$\sum_i x_s^i \leqslant \sum_j y_s^j + \sum_i w_s^i \qquad s = 0, 1, \ldots, S. \tag{2.3}$$

If all production sets Y^j and consumption sets C^i are convex, then the set of physically feasible allocations is convex. Under standard assumptions it is compact and non-empty.

Equilibrium of production and exchange

Physical feasibility ignores budget constraints altogether. In particular, it allows arbitrary allocations of individual consumption across states, subject only to the aggregate constraints (2.3). The idea of a stock-market economy is that such allocations are only possible through holdings of portfolios of shares of stock in the firms – the θ_{ij} of chapter 1. The new aspect is that trading in shares is introduced to enable consumers to choose, under an overall budget constraint, the portfolio of shares which induces the most preferred state distribution of consumption. The stock market acts as a partial substitute for insurance markets (for markets where claims to 'consumption contingent on state s' could be bought or sold in period 0).

Let the initial holdings of shares be denoted $\bar{\theta}_{ij} \geqslant 0$, with $\Sigma_i \bar{\theta}_{ij} = 1$ for each j; and let $p = (p_1, \ldots, p_j, \ldots, p_J)$ in R^J_+ denote a vector of stock prices. The final holdings are denoted θ_{ij}, elements of the $I \times J$ matrix Θ. It will be understood that final holders of shares finance the investments $y^j_0 \leqslant 0$, so that the total outlay of shareholders is $p_j - y^j_0 \geqslant p_j$.[19] The budget set of consumer i is then described by the $S + 1$ constraints

$$x^i_0 + \sum_j \theta_{ij}(p_j - y^j_0) \leqslant w^i_0 + \sum_j \bar{\theta}_{ij} p_j \tag{2.4}$$

$$x^i_s \leqslant w^i_s + \sum_j \theta_{ij} y^j_s \qquad s = 1, \ldots, S. \tag{2.5}$$

In this formulation, all savings are held in the form of equity. However, it could happen that a particular firm yields a state-independent return (output) so that its shares reduce to default-free bonds.

Let consumer preferences be monotone increasing in x^i_0 and non-decreasing in x^i_s, $s = 1, \ldots, S$.[20] Then all constraints (2.4) and (2.5) may be taken as equalities, defining x^i_s as a linear function of $\theta_i = (\theta_{i1}, \ldots, \theta_{iJ})$, given the prices p and production plans y. Consumer preferences among portfolios are then easily inferred from preferences among consumption plans.[21] In particular, continuity and convexity of preferences are preserved.[22]

Note finally that, when (2.4) and (2.5) hold for all i, with $\Sigma_i \theta_{ij} \leqslant 1$ for all j, then (2.3) is automatically verified for all s.[23]

One may then define an *equilibrium of production and exchange* (EPE) as a triple (y, p, Θ) such that:

(i) For each i, θ_i is best for i subject to (2.4) and (2.5), given y and p
(ii) For each j, $\Sigma_i \theta_{ij} = 1$
(iii) For each j, $y^j \in Y^j$ and y^j is best for firm j over Y^j, at (y, p, Θ).

This definition is still incomplete, because I have not explained what is meant by 'y^j is best for firm j over Y^j, at (y, p, Θ)' – a task to which I shall turn presently. But the nature of the equilibrium concept is clear: (i) each consumer chooses an optimal portfolio, given the share prices p and production plans y: (ii) the stock market is in equilibrium; and (iii) each firm is in equilibrium, given the overall ownership structure Θ, the stock prices p and the production plans of all other firms y^k, $k \neq j$ (here represented as y to economize notation). This is a Nash equilibrium, where each agent carries out a decision which is optimal for that agent, given the decisions of all other agents and the market signal (p).

The Pareto principle

The difficult point is of course to define 'decision criteria for business firms', that is what is 'best for j given (y,p,Θ)'. I have surveyed elsewhere (Drèze 1982) the abundant literature addressed to that topic and falling essentially under three headings, namely:

(i) Maximization of the market value p_j of the firm
(ii) Optimality with respect to the preferences of the shareholders, due account being taken of their ownership fractions θ_{ij}
(iii) Maximization of the expected value of a utility function specific to the firm (or to its management).

And I have argued that the three approaches are nested in the sense that each of them yields a decision criterion which is in general more specific than the previous one, yet consistent with it. (That is, the three approaches yield successively sharper partial orderings, which never conflict with one another.)

The first criterion is unambiguous only in the special and unrealistic case where there exist S firms with linearly independent production plans – so that insurance prices for all states can be inferred from stock prices. But in that case, all shareholders agree about an optimal production plan, and criterion (i) coincides with criterion (ii).

More generally, if there are fewer linearly independent assets than states, shareholders disagree about the ordering of production plans for firm j.[24] Indeed, each shareholder i $(\theta_{ij} > 0)$ will have an ordering on Y^j defined at (y,p,Θ) by

$$\hat{y}^j \succ_i y^j \quad \text{if and only if} \quad x^i + \theta_{ij}(\hat{y}^j - y^j) \succ_i x^i. \tag{2.6}$$

That is, each shareholder i will rank production plans for firm j on the basis of his own consumption preferences, using (2.4) and (2.5) to assess the impact on his own consumption plan of a change from y^j to $\hat{y}^j$. Unless the preferred sets of all shareholders are supported by a common hyperplane, individual rankings will diverge.[25]

The weakest and most general principle for aggregating shareholders preferences is the Pareto principle.[26]

Definition 2.1 (Pareto principle)

(i) $\hat{y}^j$ is better for j than y^j at (y,p,Θ) if and only if $\hat{y}^j >_i y^j$ according to (2.6) for all i with $\theta_{ij}>0$.
(ii) y^j is best for j over Y^j at (y,p,Θ) if and only if Y^j does not contain any $\hat{y}^j$ better than y^j according to (i).

This minimal requirement of group rationality states that y^j cannot be best, if there exists a feasible alternative $\hat{y}^j$ which *every* shareholder prefers (strictly). Clearly, a firm could not be regarded as being 'in equilibrium' at y^j if a unanimously preferred $\hat{y}^j$ existed. But this requirement is weak, because it induces only a *partial ordering*, leaving many alternatives in the optimal set.

In spite of its lack of selectivity (of definiteness), the Pareto principle is interesting because it embodies a minimal requirement of efficiency. Furthermore, my main interest in this book is to discuss the relationships between labour and capital, and much emphasis has been placed in the implicit contracts literature on the implications of the Pareto principle for labour contracts. Also, equilibria of production and exchange for the Pareto principle provide a natural reference for comparisons with labour management. Accordingly, it is worth while to record the following result, which is close in spirit to those presented in Drèze (1974b).

Theorem 2.1

Under standard assumptions, there exists an equilibrium of production and exchange for the Pareto principle.

The assumptions (convexity and boundedness) and the proof are given in appendix 2. The theorem asserts the logical consistency of our definition of an EPE, when all firms make choices compatible with the Pareto principle. It should be stressed, however, that Pareto efficiency is only claimed for each firm *conditionally* on the overall ownership structure and the production plans of the remaining firms. Simultaneous changes in the production plans of several firms, or simultaneous changes in the ownership structure and the production plans, or changes in the production plan of a firm accompanied by side payments,[27] might bring about improvements in the situations of all consumers. Our Nash Pareto optima need not be overall Pareto optima.[28]

The control principle

From a positive viewpoint, the Pareto principle suffers from an additional drawback, namely that consultation of shareholders is unwieldy, expensive and demanding. Its application would require an elaborate exchange of information about alternative production plans and about rankings of those plans by shareholders.[29] We do not observe anything of the kind in business practice outside family concerns or partnerships. In larger organizations, we observe instead delegation of authority by the shareholders to a board of directors, and again by the board of directors to managers. On major issues, the board of directors submits decisions to a specific vote of approval at a general assembly of shareholders. And the board periodically requests general endorsement of its own decisions by such a vote. Although boards of directors typically operate under statutory provisions allowing for some form of majority rule, consensus is typically desired, and is often reached through compromise; or else the intransitivities of majority voting are avoided by assigning a privileged role to the chairman.[30]

Without aiming at detailed descriptive realism, I propose to capture the gist of these organizational principles in a formal definition, labelled the control principle. The definition is of necessity somewhat complex, yet the underlying idea is simple. In order for a production plan $\hat{y}^j$ to be preferred by firm j over an alternative plan y^j, that decision must be approved by all the directors and by a majority of shareholders. Alternatively stated, the decision must be approved by a majority of shareholders including all the directors (who are thus treated as veto players). In the formal definition, the board of directors is labelled the control group, and is denoted $\mathscr{P}^j$ (for firm j).

The strength of the definition lies in the fact that the composition of the control group is allowed to depend upon the ownership of the firm.

Such a requirement is only natural. For instance, if a firm were owned by a single individual, then the control group should consist precisely of that individual, and no one else should have a say in the decisions of the firm (except through managerial delegation, about which more later). In the model under consideration, ownership is endogenous, reflecting portfolio choices. It would thus be illogical to define the control group *a priori* and independently of the endogenous portfolio choices.[31]

Of course, the manner in which the control group is related to the ownership of the firm must be specified. I treat that specification as an institutional given, which belongs in the primitive data defining the economy, on a par with the technological possibilities or the tastes and endowments of the consumers. That specification takes the form of a correspondence, associating with every ownership matrix Θ a subset of shareholders $\mathscr{I}^j(\Theta)$ with $\theta_{ij}>0$ for all i in $\mathscr{I}^j(\Theta)$, $j=1, \ldots, J$.

Obviously, majority groups of shareholders also reflect the ownership of the firm. They are denoted $\hat{\mathscr{I}}^j$ in the following definition.

Definition 2.2 (control principle)

Given the ownership matrix Θ, there exists for each firm j a unique non-empty subset $\mathscr{I}^j(\Theta)$ of $\{1, \ldots, I\}$, with $\theta_{ij}>0$ for all i in $\mathscr{I}^j(\Theta)$, called the *control group*; and

(i) $\hat{y}^j$ is better for j than y^j at (y,p,Θ) if and only if $\hat{y}^j \succ_i y^j$ according to (2.6) for all i in some (any) majority group including $\mathscr{I}^j(\Theta)$, that is for all i in some (any) subset $\hat{\mathscr{I}}^j$ of $\{1, \ldots, I\}$ with $\Sigma_i(\theta_{ij}: i \in \hat{\mathscr{I}}^j) > 1/2$ and $\mathscr{I}^j(\Theta) \subseteq \hat{\mathscr{I}}^j$.

(ii) y^j is best for j over Y^j at (y,p,Θ) if and only if Y^j does not contain any $\hat{y}^j$ better than y^j according to (i).

Remark

The definition clearly implies that $\hat{y}^j$ could be better than y^j through some majority group $\hat{\mathscr{I}}^j$, and $\tilde{y}^j$ could be better than $\hat{y}^j$ through *another* majority group $\hat{\hat{\mathscr{I}}}^j$; but the presence of $\mathscr{I}^j(\Theta)$ in both groups then precludes that y^j be better than $\tilde{y}^j$, according to the definition.

This definition obviously induces a *partial ordering* only. A special case with complete ordering would obtain if $\mathscr{I}^j(\Theta)$ consisted of a single individual i with $\theta_{ij} > 1/2$. More generally, the majority rule could be amended to recognize absentee ownership. Instead of requiring $\Sigma_i(\theta_{ij}: i \in \hat{\mathscr{I}}^j) > 1/2$, one could require $\Sigma_i(\theta_{ij}: i \in \hat{\mathscr{I}}^j) > \alpha_j(\Theta)$, with $\alpha_j(\Theta) \leqslant 1/2$ indicating the ownership fraction needed for a majority, given the ownership structure. For instance,

$$\alpha_j(\Theta) = \tfrac{1}{2}\Sigma_i(\theta_{ij}: i \ni \theta_{ij} \geqslant 0.01)$$

if only shareholders owning 1 per cent or more of the shares attend general meetings; and so on.

An interesting property of the control principle is that it covers two standard approaches; namely: the Pareto principle, which is obtained by defining $\mathscr{I}^j(\Theta)$ as the set of all consumers owning a positive fraction of the firm; and the definition of a 'utility function for the firm' through the utility function of a shareholder-manager (who never sells *all* his shares), in which case $\mathscr{I}^j(\Theta) = \{i\}$ for some i identically in Θ. Also, the control principle never violates the (weaker) Pareto principle.

Existence of an equilibrium for definition 2.2 follows from a simple assumption about the control group. (Note that Θ is a point in the Euclidean space R^{IJ}.)

Assumption CC (continuity of control)

For all i and j, the set of ownership matrices Θ such that i belongs to $\mathscr{I}^j(\Theta)$ is closed.

Alternative statements of assumption CC are given in appendix 2. The assumption says that, if i belongs to $\mathscr{I}^j(\Theta)$ for every ownership matrix Θ^v in a sequence converging to $\bar{\Theta}$, then i belongs to $\mathscr{I}^j(\bar{\Theta})$. For example, if you belong to a board of directors whenever you own *more than* 5 per cent of the shares, then you should also belong when you own *exactly* 5 per cent. Examples of admissible rules include those defining the control group as follows: all shareholders holding at least α per cent of the shares, the n leading shareholders, or the leading shareholders owning together at least β per cent of the shares (with appropriate tie-breaking rules).

Theorem 2.2

Under standard assumptions and assumption CC, there exists an equilibrium of production and exchange for definition 2.2.

The proof is given in appendix 2.

Generalizations

Two natural generalizations of the control principle are worth mentioning, namely multistage control and delegation. The idea of *multistage control* is to replace the unanimity requirement within the control group by a majority voting rule, with a set of veto players forming a proper subset of the control group and defined in accordance with the continuity assumption CC. (Majority voting with veto right for leading shareholder(s) provides an example.) As for *delegation*, it consists in vesting with the control group final authority for some decisions, while still submitting other decisions to approval by a majority of shareholders. For instance, one could specify that choices between plans which do not differ too much from each other are deferred to the control group, without interference from the general assembly. The requirements imposed on delegation for the purposes of an existence proof are natural enough: the set of production plans over which authority is delegated should be convex, and should depend continuously (if at all) upon other variables (like the reference plan, the stock prices and the decisions of other firms). When multistage delegation is introduced, it is subjected to the equally natural requirement that any group is only allowed to delegate its own final authority, to a subgroup whose composition satisfies again the continuity assumption CC. The natural next step would call for looking at delegation as a principal-agent problem and drawing on the abundant literature regarding that problem (see for example Hart and Holmström 1988).

Vote trading and side payments

In earlier analyses of stockholders equilibria, much emphasis was placed on the possibility of vote trading, that is on the possibility of transfers of current consumption among shareholders (side payments); see Drèze (1974b), Gevers (1974) and Grossman and Hart (1979).[32] This possibility has obvious normative advantages and positive limitations. It was also found to have powerful analytical implications.

The normative advantages are well known in the theory of public goods.[33] In our context, they derive from the possibility of making a change in the production plan of firm j which is not, as such, Pareto improving; but which becomes Pareto improving when accompanied by transfers of current consumption among shareholders, whereby those who favour the change compensate those who disfavour it, in such a way that everybody is made better off.

Going back to condition (2.6) and definition 2.1, consider a set of transfers $t^i = (t_0^i, 0, \ldots, 0)$ in R^{S+1}. Write t for the vector $(t^1, \ldots, t^i, \ldots, t^I)$ in $R^{I(S+1)}$; and T^j for the set of such vectors satisfying the zero-sum condition

$$\sum_i (t^i\colon i \ni \theta_{ij} > 0) = 0.$$

Each shareholder i $(\theta_{ij} > 0)$ will have an ordering on $Y^j \times T^j$ defined at (y,p,Θ) by

$$(\hat{y}^j, \hat{t}) \succ_i (y^j, 0) \quad \text{if and only if} \quad x^i + \hat{t}^i + \theta_{ij}(\hat{y}^j - y^j) \succ_i x^i. \tag{2.7}$$

One can then extend the Pareto principle to the case of side payments as follows.

Definition 2.3 (Pareto principle with side payments)

(i) $\hat{y}^j$ is better for j than y^j at (y,p,Θ) if and only if there exists a transfer vector $\hat{t}$ in T^j such that $(\hat{y}^j, \hat{t}) \succ_i (y^j, 0)$ according to (2.7) for all i with $\theta_{ij} > 0$.

(ii) y^j is best for j over Y^j at (y,p,Θ) if and only if Y^j does not contain any $\hat{y}^j$ better than y^j according to (i).

Remark

Clearly, if y^j is best for j according to definition 2.3, then it is also best for j according to definition 2.1.

The first part of definition 2.3 requires that a Pareto-improving transfer vector $\hat{t}$ should *exist*; it does not require that the transfers be *carried out*. That distinction becomes irrelevant in the second part, which asserts that y^j is best if any only if there exists *no* alternative $\hat{y}^j$, and transfer vector $\hat{t}$ in T^j, that would make everybody better off. The idea is that such an alternative, and the associated transfers, would be carried out if available.

Some analytical implications of definition 2.3 are developed in Drèze (1974b). If y^j is best for j over Y^j at (y,p,Θ), there exists for each i with $\theta_{ij} > 0$ a vector of *personalized insurance prices* $\pi^i = (1, \pi_1^i, \ldots, \pi_s^i, \ldots, \pi_S^i)$ in R_+^{S+1}, such that:

(i) $(\hat{y}^j,\hat{t}) >_i (y^j,0)$ according to (2.7) implies

$$\hat{t}^i + \theta_{ij}\pi^i(\hat{y}^j - y^j) = \hat{t}^i + \theta_{ij}[\hat{y}^j_0 - y^j_0 + \Sigma_s\pi^i_s(\hat{y}^j_s - y^j_s)] > 0$$

(ii) $y^j_0 + \Sigma_s y^j_s(\Sigma_i\theta_{ij}\pi^i_s) = \Sigma_i\theta_{ij}\pi^i y^j \geqslant \Sigma_i\theta_{ij}\pi^i\hat{y}^j$ for all $\hat{y}^j$ in Y^j.

Here $\pi^i_s (s \geqslant 1)$ is interpreted as the insurance premium (per unit) which i would just be willing to pay for an infinitesimal amount of insurance on state s (for an infinitesimal claim contingent on state s). Under differentiability, π^i_s is i's marginal rate of substitution between x^i_0 and x^i_s. For firm j, $\Sigma_i\theta_{ij}\pi^i$ is a vector of *shadow prices* at which the value of production plan y^j is maximal over Y^j. The definition of these shadow prices as a weighted sum of personalized prices, $\Sigma_i\theta_{ij}\pi^i$, is an extension to our context of the Lindahl-Samuelson conditions for efficient production of public goods.[34]

There are also some general equilibrium implications. Not only can one prove existence of an equilibrium of production and exchange with transfers – called 'stockholders equilibrium' in Drèze (1974b, theorem 3.4.1). One can also prove that every Pareto-optimal allocation satisfying (2.3) and (2.5) is a stockholders equilibrium[35] (Drèze 1974b, theorem 3.4.2), although the converse is not true (as revealed by the examples in Drèze 1974b, section IV). More interestingly, one can define a decentralized dynamic process converging to stockholders equilibria (Drèze 1974b, theorem 5.3). The process has a natural interpretation. Every morning, the stock exchange meets and reaches a state of *competitive equilibrium*. That is, each consumer ends up holding an optimal portfolio, and $\Sigma_i\theta_{ij} = 1$ for all j; conditions (i) and (ii) in the earlier definition of an equilibrium of production and exchange are satisfied. Each afternoon, all firms in succession hold stockholders meetings; side payments among shareholders are permitted, and each firm chooses by the unanimity rule a plan which is best according to definition 2.3 (with the required transfers actually taking place).[36] The same procedure is repeated the next day. New transactions may occur on the stock exchange, because the plans of the firms and the endowments of the consumers have changed. Stockholders meetings bring together in the afternoon new sets of shareholders, who revise the plans of the firms. Under standard assumptions, either the process terminates at a stockholders equilibrium, or the limit of any convergent subsequence of allocations is a stockholders equilibrium. Of course, such a stockholders equilibrium is an equilibrium of production and exchange, relative to the final endowments reflecting the sequence of transfers and stock-market transactions.

The stability argument does not carry over to the case where production decisions are governed by the control principle. Indeed, stability is obtained because the utilities of consumers increase monotonically along the process: production plans are revised according to the Pareto principle, and trading on the stock market is always utility improving. In contrast, the control principle allows revisions of the production plans which are detrimental to a *minority* of stockholders. (And it is not known *ex ante* whom the minority may consist of.)

One limitation of equilibria with side payments is that they postulate unlimited communication, and ability to form coalitions, among *all* shareholders of a firm. It would be more realistic to consider side payments among major shareholders only - for instance among members of the control group. Unfortunately, the existence argument of appendix 2 does not apply in that case.[37] It should, however, apply to an intermediate situation, where side payments are considered among the shareholders forming the majority which approves a change in the production plan. At least, that group is identified, and revealed willing to form a voting coalition. That idea is embodied in the following definition.

Definition 2.4 (control principle with side payments)

Let $\mathscr{I}^j(\Theta)$ be as defined in definition 2.2. Then

(i) $\hat{y}^j$ is better for j than y^j at (y,p,Θ) if and only if there exists a majority group $\hat{\mathscr{I}}^j$ including $\mathscr{I}^j(\Theta)$, and a transfer vector $\hat{t}$ with $\Sigma_i(\hat{t}^i : i \in \hat{\mathscr{I}}^j) = 0$ such that $(\hat{y}^j,\hat{t}) \succ_i (y^j,0)$ according to (2.7) for all i in $\hat{\mathscr{I}}^j$.

(ii) y^j is best for j over Y^j at (y,p,Θ) if and only if Y^j does not contain any $\hat{y}^j$ better than y^j according to (i).

Remark

Clearly, if y^j is best for j according to definition 2.4, then it is also best for j according to definition 2.2, but not necessarily according to definition 2.3.

Although I have not attempted to do so formally, I would expect existence of an equilibrium of production and exchange for definition 2.4 to follow from standard assumptions and assumption CC.

Notes

1 Resources are discovered or accidentally destroyed, living habits take unpredicted turns, technological knowledge develops through research and experimentation, and so on.
2 This is the model of so-called 'technological uncertainty', introduced by Arrow (1953) and developed by Debreu (1959, chapter 7); see also Baudier (1959), Borch (1962), or the expository survey by Guesnerie and de Montbrial (1974). In that model, the variability of prices, incomes, profits and so on is derived from the primitive uncertainty about the environment. More recently, the 'economics of information' have been concerned with the additional uncertainties created by imperfect dissemination of existing information about the environment; see for example Hirshleifer and Riley (1979) for emphasis on the distinction and further references.
3 A spot market may be viewed as a degenerate insurance market; a futures market is a market where sets of insurance contracts are traded jointly.
4 The economic evaluation differs from actuarial evaluation. Whereas the latter reflects only the probability of an event, the former reflects both that probability and the utility of the economic consequences. See for example Drèze (1971) for an elaboration of this remark.
5 See for example Arrow (1970a, chapters 5 and 10) or Drèze (1979, section 2) for further remarks.
6 This property is at the root of the original contribution by Arrow (1953).
7 For recent surveys see Radner (1982) or Drèze (1982).
8 Meade continues: 'This presumably is a main reason why we find risk-bearing capital hiring labour rather than risk-bearing labour hiring capital.' More on this later.
9 That literature goes back to the seminal papers by Azariadis (1975), Baily (1974) and Gordon (1974). It has flourished in a number of directions, some of which were surveyed by Azariadis (1983), Ito (1982) and more recently by Rosen (1985) or Hart and Holmström (1988). The first, and to the best of my knowledge the only, general equilibrium formulation is due to Holmström (1983).
10 See however Peters (1983) for a step in that direction.
11 See for example Becker (1964).
12 The major exception concerns transportation equipment (aeroplanes, ships) which are easily transferred to alternative routes, with interesting implications brought out in Baumol, Panzar and Willig (1982).
13 Compare Drèze (1987b, p. 20) and Drèze (1985c, pp. 282–3).

14 No mention was made there of the need for financial capital, because credit-worthiness is not an issue under complete certainty.

15 This symmetry was already recognized, albeit along a different route, in a paper by Miyazaki and Neary (1983).

16 See for example Mossin (1977) or Drèze (1974b, 1982) for further details.

17 A streamlined version of section 2.2 has appeared as Drèze (1985b).

18 See figures 1 and 2 in Drèze (1974b).

19 Thus dividends paid in period 0 are subsumed under w_0^i, $i = 1, \ldots, I$.

20 Strict monotonicity in x_s^i would rule out cases where i regards state s as impossible.

21 Say, $V^i(\theta_i) = \text{def } u^i(x^i(\theta_i|p,y))$, with $x^i(\theta_i|p,y)$ defined by (2.4) and (2.5).

22 Strict convexity is not preserved, when production plans are linearly dependent; monotonicity need not be preserved, when $y_0^j < 0$.

23 $\Sigma_i\theta_{ij} < 1$ creates no difficulty when Y^j is convex with $0 \in Y^j$; indeed, $y^j \in Y^j$ then implies $(\Sigma_i\theta_{ij})y^j \in Y^j$.

24 Also, in that case, the effect on stock prices of a change in y^j is not known in advance; and it is no longer true that all shareholders benefit from an increase in p_j (see Drèze 1974b, section VI (3)).

25 A common hyperplane would exist if a full set of insurance prices could be inferred from the asset prices p, but otherwise not (except by accident).

26 For technical reasons revealed in appendix 2, I am using here the strong form of the Pareto principle instead of the more usual form where indifference of some, but not all, consumers is allowed.

27 Side payments are discussed later in this section.

28 See Drèze (1974b) for details and examples. At an interior solution with differentiable preferences, an EPE for definition 2.1 satisfies productive efficiency; more generally, even that property may fail to hold.

29 See however note 36.

30 Thus if the chairman decides on the issues put to a vote, and knows the preferences of his colleagues, he is *de facto* a veto player.

31 That is also a drawback of approaches whereby decisions are entrusted to a manager, assumed to act according to his own consumption preferences, *irrespective of who owns the firm.*

32 See Grossman and Hart (1979, p. 301) for an explicit interpretation of side payments in terms of vote trading.

33 See for example Milleron (1972).

34 See Milleron (1972) for a derivation of these conditions.

35 Conditions (2.4) are no longer binding when transfers are allowed; the aggregate condition (2.3), with $s = 0$, suffices.

36 That choice could be achieved by means of the so-called MDP procedure for public goods: see Malinvaud (1971) or Drèze and de la Vallée Poussin (1971).

37 I am grateful to John Geanakoplos for bringing the relevant technical difficulty to my attention.

CHAPTER 3

Stock-market Economies with Labour Contracts

3.1 Labour contracts

I will now introduce labour formally into the model of chapter 2. In the same way that attention was confined there to a single physical commodity, I shall consider here a single type of labour. Let $z^j = (z_0^j, z_1^j, \ldots, z_S^j)$ in R_+^{S+1} denote a vector of labour inputs for firm j, where as usual z_0^j denotes the quantity of labour used in period 0, and z_s^j the quantity used in period 1 under state s. A production plan for firm j is now a pair of vectors (y^j, z^j). The production set Y^j in $R^{2(S+1)}$ is the set of such vectors which are technologically feasible. All components of the plan are non-negative, except possibly for y_0^j, which is now unrestricted as to sign. (With the use of labour in period 0 is typically associated a positive output; from this must be subtracted the investment realized in period 0; the algebraic sum of these two terms can be positive, negative or null.[1])

The production set Y^j defines simultaneously two aspects of the technology. On the one hand, it describes how output is related to contemporaneous labour input, both in period 0 and in period 1 under every state. On the other hand, it describes how future production possibilities are related to current investment. That relationship is a complex one, as it combines an effect due to the scale of investment, and an effect due to the choice by the firm of a state distribution of production possibilities.

In the example of section 2.2, growing tomatoes requires the use of labour both in period 0 (to prepare the soil, to set the plants and so on) and in period 1 (to pick the tomatoes and so on). The production possibilities for period 1 (a set of feasible labour–output pairs) depend upon the state (rain or sunshine), and upon the nature and level of investment in period 0 (whether greenhouse or outdoors, what acreage and such like).

Standard models of economies with labour contracts have abstracted from the investment aspect, and treated the production possibilities in period 1 state s as given – say by a function $f_s^j(z_s^j)$ relating output to labour input there. That formulation is a special case of the more general model used here, where the investment decision of period 0 matters, both in nature and in level.[2] In particular, there is scope for choosing between more capital-intensive and more labour-intensive techniques. In the real world such choices are made, and are responsive to the degree of uncertainty; for instance, investment in fixed capital to economize on labour is more attractive when the probability of using the capital at full capacity is higher.

The decision to use a capital-intensive, labour-saving technology is also influenced by the relative costs of capital and labour. These costs must be assessed over the lifetime of the equipment, here collapsed to period 1 alone. With all the physical investment taking place in period 0, its cost is well defined. But labour will be used in period 1 as well. Is the associated cost known in period 0?

Two polar situations have retained attention. At one extreme, labour is a 'variable factor'. Each firm 'hires' labour on a spot market, both in period 0 and in period 1 under state s. With competitive market clearing, each firm contemplates the possibility of hiring as much labour as it wants, but the price (wage) will depend upon the state. In the absence of contingent markets, the future wages must be fore-casted. In practice, this typically results in a multiplication of the number of states *relevant* to the investment decision of each firm. For instance, a firm engaged in tomato farming could, in the framework of chapter 2, be concerned only about the contingencies affecting the yield and price of tomatoes. Now it becomes concerned about all the contin-gencies influencing the wage level.

Similarly, workers may contemplate the possibility of selling as much labour as they want, but the wage will again depend upon the state. This may result in considerable uncertainty about real income, since the market clearing wage may, in bad states, drop to very low levels.

It was noted by Azariadis (1975), Baily (1974) and Gordon (1974) that better arrangements for sharing the risks associated with wage uncertainty could be devised, because the attitudes towards risks of firms and workers differ. This is the starting-point of the theory of 'implicit labour contracts'[3] and of the second polar situation. Consider the alternative arrangement where firms contract with workers for the two periods *simultaneously*, and no spot market is organized in period 1. (This is again an extreme case, since more generally spot markets and longer-term contracts will coexist; with overlapping generations of workers, a spot market for new contracts opens in each period.) A contract will stipulate the quantity of labour to be supplied in period 0 and in period 1 under each state; and it will stipulate the corresponding compensation. For instance, if firm j contracted with a single worker, the quantities of labour would be given by $z^j = (z_0^j, z_1^j, \ldots, z_S^j)$. Denote the total compensation by $t^j = (t_0^j, t_1^j, \ldots, t_S^j)$, thereby defining implicitly the wage rates t_s^j/z_s^j, $s = 0, 1, \ldots, S$. A labour contract is then a pair of vectors (z^j, t^j) in $R_+^{2(S+1)}$, specifying fully the workload and the income of the worker. The firm signing such a contract makes a joint decision about its production (and investment) plan (y^j, z^j) and its labour contract (z^j, t^j) - say altogether $d^j = (y^j, z^j, t^j)$. The shareholders of the firm then contribute or receive net amounts $y^j - t^j$; in particular, $y_s^j - t_s^j$, $s = 1, \ldots, S$, defines the vector of 'dividends' in period 1 under all states.

The extension to several workers can be modelled in a number of ways, even with a single type of labour. In particular, it matters whether the firm offers a single contract, the same for all workers, or whether it offers a multiplicity of contracts among which workers may choose.[4]

The rationale for a multiplicity of contracts would be that risk preferences and income–leisure preferences vary among workers, even when labour is homogeneous in production. Tailoring contracts to individual preferences is then conducive to further efficiency gains. On the other hand, these gains do not come free, because individual contracts are costly to write and administer, lead to unequal treatment *ex post*, and so on. Typically, the number of different contracts for similar labour in a given firm is very small, and is covered by simple clauses (like seniority). I shall here restrict attention to the simpler case where each firm offers a single contract.[5]

It is then pedagogically suggestive to consider first a model where individual workers supply a *fraction* of the firm's labour contract, say

ζ_{ij} for worker i in firm j.[6] Equilibrium then requires $\Sigma_i \zeta_{ij} = 1$ for all j. The associated workload and income are of course $\zeta_{ij} z^j$ and $\zeta_{ij} t^j$, respectively. This formulation leads to a symmetrical presentation of the equilibrium conditions on the stock market and on the market for labour contracts.

There is of course a lack of realism in treating the fractions ζ_{ij} as continuous variables, and in letting all workers contract simultaneously with several firms.[7] This ignores the indivisibilities of labour time, transportation and so on, and suggests that a worker may in fact 'put a small bit of his effort into a large number of different jobs', contrary to Meade's realistic observation. The obvious alternative is to impose that each worker supplies a fixed quantity of labour to a single firm. That formulation has been adopted by some authors, who typically restore convexity by introducing a continuum of workers.[8] Both formulations carry their own limitations, but remain instructive under appropriate care in interpreting results. My choice here is dictated by convenience and suggestiveness of presentation.

Proceeding as in chapter 2, I shall first consider in section 3.2 a model where the decisions of firms are simply Pareto efficient from the viewpoint of their members – here shareholders and workers. Thereafter in section 3.3 I shall take a more positive approach, using again the control principle to describe the decisions of firms, and introducing the realistic consideration that hiring decisions at time 0 are under the firm's control. (The significance of that consideration is brought out in section 3.3.) Some properties of Pareto-efficient contracts are discussed in section 3.4.

3.2 Equilibria with Pareto-efficient labour contracts

Production, exchange and labour contracts

For the purpose of extending the Pareto principle, I simply put together the elements introduced in section 3.1, obtaining the following model. Each firm j has a production set Y^j in the space $R^{2(S+1)}$ of production plans (y^j, z^j). The set Y^j has standard properties (convexity, possibility of inaction, bounded outputs given finite inputs). The firm chooses a *decision* $d^j = (y^j, z^j, t^j)$ with $t^j = (t^j_0, t^j_1, \ldots, t^j_S)$ in R^{S+1}_+ defining the total compensation of labour, subject to the limited liability conditions

$$y_s^j - t_s^j \geqslant 0 \qquad s = 1, \ldots, S. \tag{3.1}$$

(Limited liability is a natural constraint, considering that negative dividends are not easily collected from anonymous shareholders.) The set of *feasible decisions*, for which (y^j, z^j) belongs to Y^j and (3.1) holds, is denoted D^j.

Each consumer $i = 1, \ldots, I$ has a consumption set C^i in the space $R_+^{2(S+1)}$ of *consumption and labour plans* (x^i, z^i). That set is completely ordered by the preference relation $\succsim_i$ – continuous, convex, monotone increasing in x^i (strictly so in x_0^i) and decreasing in z^i. The consumer has initial resources w^i in the interior of R_+^{S+1} and initial holdings of shares $\bar{\theta}_i = (\bar{\theta}_{i1}, \ldots, \bar{\theta}_{iJ})$. The consumer chooses a portfolio of shares of stock $\theta_i = (\theta_{i1}, \ldots, \theta_{iJ})$, $1 \geqslant \theta_{ij} \geqslant 0$, and a portfolio of *shares of labour contracts* $\zeta_i = (\zeta_{i1}, \ldots, \zeta_{iJ})$, $1 \geqslant \zeta_{ij} \geqslant 0$, where the jth labour contract is defined by the pair (z^j, t^j) from the decision d^j. The resulting consumption and labour plan is defined by:

$$z^i = \sum_j \zeta_{ij} z^j \tag{3.2}$$

$$x_0^i = w_0^i + \sum_j \bar{\theta}_{ij} p_j + \sum_j \zeta_{ij} t_0^j + \sum_j \theta_{ij} (y_0^j - t_0^j - p_j) \tag{3.3}$$

$$x_s^i = w_s^i + \sum_j \zeta_{ij} t_s^j + \sum_j \theta_{ij} (y_s^j - t_s^j) \qquad s = 1, \ldots, S \tag{3.4}$$

where p_j in R_+ is the market value of firm j on the stock exchange. On the right-hand side of (3.4), we find the three components of household incomes: initial assets, wages and dividends.

The equalities (3.2)–(3.4) are linear in (θ_i, ζ_i) given $d^j, p_j, j = 1, \ldots, J$. It follows that the preferences $\succsim_i$ on C^i induce a preference relation on the set of admissible portfolios (θ_i, ζ_i). (Admissible portfolios are such that $x_0^i \geqslant 0$). That induced preference relation is continuous and convex.[9]

An *equilibrium of production, exchange and labour contracts* (EPEC) consists of a price vector $p \in R_+^J$, a set of decisions d^j, $j = 1, \ldots, J$, and a set of portfolios (θ_i, ζ_i), $i = 1, \ldots, I$; in short, a quadruple (p, d, Θ, Z) such that

(i) For each i, the portfolio (θ_i, ζ_i) is admissible and induces via (3.2)–(3.4) a consumption and labour plan $(x^i, z^i) \in C^i$, and there exists no alternative admissible portfolio $(\hat{\theta}_i, \hat{\zeta}_i)$ such that the induced plan $(\hat{x}^i, \hat{z}^i)$ belongs to C^i with $(\hat{x}^i, \hat{z}^i) \succ_i (x^i, z^i)$.

(ii) For each j, $\Sigma_i \theta_{ij} = 1$ and $\Sigma_i \zeta_{ij} = 1$.

(iii) For each j, $d^j \in D^j$ and the decision d^j is best for firm j over D^j at (p, d, Θ, Z).

That definition extends naturally the definition of an EPE in chapter 2 – and is similarly incomplete, pending a precise definition of what is meant by the statement 'the decision d^j is best for firm j . . .'. But the nature of the equilibrium is the same, with (i) reflecting equilibrium choices by the consumers, (ii) market equilibrium and (iii) equilibrium decisions by the firms. Again, this is a Nash equilibrium.

Note that labour and capital are treated almost, but not quite, symmetrically in the definition of an EPEC. The difference is that shares of stock are traded on a stock market, cleared at competitive prices p. There is no price system for labour contracts. Instead, the compensation vectors t^j play that role. One may think about t_0^j, the compensation in period 0, as the 'price' of a contract $(z^j, t_1^j, \ldots, t_S^j)$, with t_0^j set competitively to clear 'the labour market of firm j'. But there are no initial holdings of labour shares, and firm j is a monopsonist on its own labour market. The 'monopsonist' element is tempered by the fact that firms compete with each other to hire labour. In equilibrium, consumers supply their labour optimally, given the labour contracts offered by the different firms; and all labour markets clear.

Existence of equilibria for the Pareto principle

There is no logical difficulty in extending the Pareto principle, as introduced in chapter 2, to the model of the present section.

Under a given portfolio (θ_i, ζ_i) and given the decisions d^k in all firms $k \neq j$, consumer i will have an ordering on the decisions d^j of firm j defined by

$$\hat{d}^j \succ_i d^j \quad \text{if and only if} \quad (\hat{x}^i, \hat{z}^i) \succ_i (x^i, z^i) \tag{3.5}$$

where

$$\hat{x}^i = x^i + \theta_{ij}(\hat{y}^j - \hat{t}^j - y^j + t^j) + \zeta_{ij}(\hat{t}^j - t^j) \tag{3.6}$$

$$\hat{z}^i = z^i + \zeta_{ij}(\hat{z}^j - z^j). \tag{3.7}$$

That is, each consumer i will rank decisions by firm j on the basis of his own preferences among consumption and labour plans, using (3.2)–(3.4) to assess the impact on his own plan of a change from d^j to $\hat{d}^j$. The definition (3.5) corresponds to (2.6), and coincides with it when $\zeta_{ij} = 0$, or when d^j and $\hat{d}^j$ include the same labour contract (and differ only as to y^j). More generally, (3.5) takes into account labour income and labour time. In practice, a particular consumer is typically concerned about d^j either as a shareholder $(\theta_{ij} > 0)$, or as a worker

($\zeta_{ij} > 0$), but seldom in both capacities simultaneously ($\theta_{ij}\zeta_{ij} > 0$). The general formulation (3.5) covers all possibilities.

Definition 2.1′ (Pareto principle with labour contracts)

(i) $\hat{d}^j$ is better for j than d^j at (p,d,Θ,Z) if and only if $\hat{d}^j >_i d^j$ according to (3.5)–(3.7) for all i with $\theta_{ij} + \zeta_{ij} > 0$.
(ii) d^j is best for j over D^j at (p,d,Θ,Z) if and only if D^j does not contain any $\hat{d}^j$ better than d^j according to (i).

This minimal requirement of group rationality states that d^j cannot be best, if there exists an alternative $\hat{d}^j$ which every shareholder and every employee prefers (strictly); that is, an alternative which all concerned (via $\theta_{ij} > 0$ or $\zeta_{ij} > 0$ or both) prefer. A firm could not be regarded as being 'in equilibrium' at d^j if a unanimously preferred $\hat{d}^j$ existed. That principle also underlies most of the literature on implicit contracts, say in the form of maximizing the expected utility of a single owner of the firm subject to a constraint on the expected utility level of identical workers, as in Holmström (1983) or Hart (1983). Still, as remarked already in connection with definiton 2.1, it is a weak requirement, inducing a partial ordering which leaves many alternatives in the optimal set.

Not surprisingly, a result analogous to that recorded in theorem 2.1 holds.

Theorem 3.1

Under standard assumptions, there exists an equilibrium of production, exchange and labour contracts for the Pareto principle.

Properties of equilibria for the Pareto principle

Theorem 3.1 asserts the logical consistency of our definition of an EPEC, when all firms make choices compatible with the Pareto principle. The formulation is quite general, and covers as special cases many of the models used in the literature on implicit labour contracts. Of course, the main interest in that literature is to derive specific properties of Pareto-efficient contracts. Some general properties are given in section 3.4. As in the case of theorem 2.1, it must be stressed that Pareto efficiency is only claimed for each firm *conditionally* on the decisions of the consumers and of the remaining firms. An EPEC is a Nash-Pareto optimum, not an *overall* (constrained) Pareto optimum (that is, not a Pareto optimum relative to the constraints (3.2)–(3.4) and physical feasibility).

It is worth noting at once that the Pareto principle of definition 2.1′ implies that each firm uses labour efficiently, under the constraints of the model. First of all, it would not be possible to obtain the same vector of outputs while using less labour either in period 0, or in period 1 under some state, without using more labour somewhere (technological efficiency). Second, any change in the production plan would make some consumer worse off, even if the division of output between workers (t^j) and shareholders ($y^j - t^j$) were simultaneously adjusted. If all workers were identical, this would also mean that in both periods and under all states the marginal product of labour is equal to the workers' marginal rate of substitution between leisure and consumption – a standard result in implicit contracts theory. When workers are not identical an aggregation problem arises, to which I return in section 3.4.

As for risk-sharing, the compensation vector t^j specified in the labour contract introduces transfers between the *group* of shareholders and the *group* of workers, both in period 0 and in period 1 conditionally on the state that obtains. The contracts thus embody a form of *mutual group insurance*, discussed at greater length in section 3.4. In this way, the diversification possibilities offered by the stock market are extended indirectly to the workers, because they engage in this form of mutual insurance with a group of shareholders displaying (at the margin) less risk aversion than would be the case in the absence of a stock market.[10]

These properties (efficient use of labour, group insurance) hold firm by firm, but not across firms. Thus it could be that the marginal product of labour in state s differs between firm k and firm j. There is a limit to the extent of this inefficiency, under additional assumptions. For instance, if the workers of each firm had identical tastes and some workers contracted simultaneously with both, then the equality between the marginal product of labour in either firm with a common leisure–consumption trade-off would imply equality of the marginal products. But that is a very special case, and in general overall efficiency in the use of labour will not hold. This should not surprise us, in a model where labour mobility between firms conditionally on the state is not introduced explicitly. Spot markets for labour in period 1 would remedy this defect to some extent, at least in the present context where hours worked are allowed to vary freely.

3.3 Equilibria of production, exchange and labour contracts

Labour demand by firms

The Pareto principle treats workers and shareholders symmetrically, and is thus equally applicable to situations where capital hires labour (capitalist firms) and to situations where labour hires capital (labour-managed firms). That property will prove convenient for comparing the two forms of organization in chapter 4. On the other hand, the theory of labour contracts was initially developed for situations where capital hires labour. The idea is that competitive markets for contracts replace competitive spot markets for labour, and firms make decisions which are optimal for capital owners under the prevailing market opportunities for hiring labour. Two simplifying assumptions pervade the existing literature known to me. The first concerns capital owners. Each firm is endowed with a well-defined utility function, which either reflects the preferences of a single owner-manager, as in Hart (1983), or is linear in profit (risk neutrality), as in Holström (1983). The second commonly used assumption is that of identical workers, which permits reliance on the simple equilibrium condition that the contracts of all firms should entail the same expected utility for the workers.

The analysis of chapter 2 suggests a natural generalization of the first assumption, namely reliance on the control principle to explain endogenously the behaviour of firms, in a stock-market economy with imperfect diversification. The new aspect is the modelling of markets for labour contracts with heterogeneous workers.

The idea that firms make optimal decisions 'under the prevailing market opportunities for hiring labour' entails in particular that firms retain control over their hiring decisions in period 0, subject to abiding with the terms of labour contracts negotiated with their employees. In equilibrium, employment at time 0 should be optimal for the firm, given the terms of the contract. (Sophisticated contract models assume that unions take into account the implications of contract terms for employment levels, but these models are developed in a partial equilibrium framework.)

The Pareto principle, as stated in definition 2.1′, does not reflect that idea; instead, it requires that no alternative employment-and-compensation scheme should be preferred by *all* consumers concerned (either as workers or as shareholders). Thus, it could be that shareholders would prefer that workers put in longer hours (at the same hourly wages), but some workers prefer not to. The Pareto principle of definition 2.1′ does not include a provision allowing the firm to hire additional workers in such cases. And the condition of labour market equilibrium ($\Sigma_i \zeta_{ij} = 1$) embodied in that definition states that employment in firm j should correspond to unconstrained labour *supply*, not to equality of unconstrained supply by workers and *demand* by the firm (given the terms of the contract).

To be specific, consider an economy with one firm and two consumers. Consumer 1 owns the firm and does not work. Consumer 2 does not own assets but supplies one unit of labour inelastically in period 0. (Period 1 is not needed for the present illustration.) Any wage level, not exceeding the output produced by one unit of labour (average product), is compatible with equilibrium (EPEC) for the Pareto principle. The only condition imposed by that concept is efficient use of labour (that is, a labour input equal to unity). Any division of output is Pareto efficient, and compatible in the example with equilibrium labour *supply*. Whereas the condition for a competitive equilibrium would be that the wage level should correspond to the marginal product of labour.

A concept capturing the spirit of competitive equilibria, in an economy with a stock market and labour contracts, should thus embody a condition of unconstrained labour demand by firms acting in the interests of their shareholders, on a par with the condition of unconstrained labour supply by workers. Equality of the supply and demand for labour and efficiency of the terms of labour contracts close the model. That is also the spirit of the existing literature on implicit labour contracts. Such an equilibrium concept can be defined, at the level of generality retained here, by relying upon the control principle to explain the decisions of firms, and in particular their labour demand. There remains only to model the negotiations about the terms of the labour contracts (working time and wages, both in period 0 and in every state of period 1).

With heterogeneous preferences among the workers, some form of group decision is involved in these negotiations. Labour unions provide an institutional framework for group decisions by workers.

Although one could easily model of a form of control principle for unions, I retain here the simpler alternative of majority voting by workers to approve the terms of labour contracts, or to define preferred alternatives. This seems to conform well to established practice. On important issues, workers are called upon to approve a prospective contract at a general assembly, where majority voting is the standard decision procedure.

Existence of equilibria for the control principle and majority voting by workers

To minimize departures from the notation used so far, one may define the *terms of a contract* by the ratios z_s^j/z_0^j, $s = 1, \ldots, S$, defining working times (or 'retention rates') in all states of period 1 relative to that of period 0, and t_s^j/z_0^j, $s = 0, 1, \ldots, S$, defining wages per unit of labour in period 0. (Thus $t_0{}^j/z_0^j$ is a wage per unit of labour in period 0; t_s^j/z_0^j, $s \geqslant 1$ is a wage in period 1 state s per unit of labour in period 0, not per unit of labour in state s; this allows in particular to compensate in state s workers who are idle then.) Let then

$$\rho^j = \frac{z^j}{z_0^j} = \left(1, \frac{z_1^j}{z_0^j}, \ldots, \frac{z_S^j}{z_0^j}\right) \qquad \tau^j = \frac{t^j}{z_0^j} = \left(\frac{t_0^j}{z_0^j}, \ldots, \frac{t_S^j}{z_0^j}\right)$$

and define a labour contract c^j as a pair $c^j = (\rho^j, \tau^j)$. A decision for firm j, $d^j = (y^j, z^j, t^j)$, may also be written as $(y^j, z_0^j\rho^j, z_0^j\tau^j)$ or as a pair $((y^j, z_0^j), c^j)$ consisting of an output and employment decision (y^j, z_0^j) and a labour contract c^j. The set of decisions compatible with the contract c^j is then defined as

$$\begin{aligned} D^j(c^j) &= \{d^j \in D^j \mid z^j = z_0^j\rho^j, t^j = z_0^j\tau^j\} \\ &= \left\{(y^j, z^j, t^j) \mid (y^j, z^j) \in Y^j,\ y_s^j - t_s^j \geqslant 0\ \forall\, s = 1, \ldots, S,\right. \\ &\qquad \left. \frac{z^j}{z_0^j} = \rho^j, \frac{t^j}{z_0^j} = \tau^j\right\}. \end{aligned} \tag{3.8}$$

To reflect the idea that firms retain control over their hiring decisions, I shall assume that *shareholders* compare alternative decisions for firm j on the basis of alternative state distributions of dividends, regarding as fixed their portfolios θ_i and aggregate labour supply z^i. (That is, shareholders consider that firm j can change its employment level without alteration of their own employment status in that firm if any.) On the other hand, I shall assume that *workers* compare terms of labour contracts in firm j on the basis of alternative state distributions of working times and wage incomes, regarding as fixed their shares of labour contracts ζ^i and aggregate property incomes $\Sigma_j \theta_{ij}(y^j - t^j)$. (When $\theta_{ij}\zeta_{ij} = 0$, these stipulations are covered by (3.5)–(3.7), but otherwise they are slightly at variance.) This amounts to assuming that firms consult shareholders on alternative state distributions of dividends, without reporting to them what employment and wage policies are associated with these dividends. Similarly, firms negotiate with workers the terms of labour contracts, without reporting to them what dividend policies are associated with these labour contracts. That formulation seems broadly consistent with the practice of capitalist firms.

An allocation for the economy is now a tuple (p,c,d,Θ,Z), and optimal choices are defined as follows.

Definition 3.1 (optimal production and employment decisions for the control principle under given labour contracts)

(i) The decision $\hat{d}^j \in D^j(c^j)$ is better for firm j than $d^j \in D^j(c^j)$, at (p,c,d,Θ,Z), if and only if there exists $\hat{\mathscr{I}}^j \subseteq \{1, \ldots, I\}$ with $\mathscr{I}^j(\Theta) \subseteq \hat{\mathscr{I}}^j$, $\Sigma_i(\Theta_{ij}: i \in \hat{\mathscr{I}}^j) > 1/2$ and, for all $i \in \hat{\mathscr{I}}^j$,

$$(x^i + \theta_{ij}(\hat{y}^j - \hat{t}^j - y^j + t^j), z^i) \succ_i (x^i, z^i). \tag{3.9}$$

(ii) The decision d^j is best for firm j over $D^j(c^j)$ at (p,c,d,Θ,Z) if and only if $D^j(c^j)$ does not contain any $\hat{d}^j$ better for j according to (i).

Definition 3.2 (optimal labour contracts for the control principle and majority voting by workers)

(i) The contract $\hat{c}^j$ is better for firm j than the contract c^j at (p,c,d,Θ,Z), if and only if there exist $\hat{d}^j \in D^j(\hat{c}^j)$ and subsets $\tilde{\mathscr{I}}^j, \hat{\mathscr{I}}^j$ of $\{1, \ldots, I\}$ such that

(a) $\Sigma_i(\zeta_{ij}: i \in \tilde{\mathscr{I}}^j) > 1/2$ and, for all $i \in \tilde{\mathscr{I}}^j$,

$$(x^i + \zeta_{ij}(\hat{t}^j - t^j), z^i + \zeta_{ij}(\hat{z}^j - z^j)) \succ_i (x^i, z^i) \tag{3.10}$$

(b) $\mathscr{I}^j(\Theta) \subseteq \hat{\mathscr{I}}^j$, $\Sigma_i(\theta_{ij}: i \in \hat{\mathscr{I}}^j) > 1/2$ and, for all $i \in \hat{\mathscr{I}}^j$,

$$(x^i + \theta_{ij}(\hat{y}^j - \hat{t}^j - y^j + t^j), z^i) \succ_i (x^i, z^i). \tag{3.11}$$

(ii) The contract c^j is best for firm j at (p,c,d,Θ,Z) if and only if there does not exist an alternative contract $\hat{c}^j$ better for firm j according to (i).[11]

The resulting equilibrium concept is labelled an *equilibrium of production, exchange and labour contracts for the control principle and majority voting by workers* (or EPEC for definitions 3.1 and 3.2). It calls for a set of feasible consumer choices (θ_i, ζ_i), a set of labour contracts c^j, a set of feasible firm decisions d^j and a vector of stock prices p, such that:

(i) For each consumer i, the choice (θ_i, ζ_i), is best over i's feasible set.
(ii) The stock market clears ($\Sigma_i \theta_{ij} = 1 \forall j$) and all the labour markets clear ($\Sigma_i \zeta_{ij} = 1 \forall j$).
(iii) For each firm j, the production and employment decision d^j is best over the feasible set $D^j(c^j)$, according to definition 3.1.
(iv) For each firm j, the labour contract c^j is best for firm j, according to definition 3.2.

Theorem 3.2

Under standard assumptions (somewhat beefed up for technical convenience) and assumption CC, there exists an equilibrium of production, exchange and labour contracts for the control principle and majority voting by workers (or EPEC for definitions 3.1 and 3.2).

The proof is presented in appendix 3, as a (tedious) extension of the proof of theorem 2.2. Although the formalism there is somewhat different, the basic ideas are the same. The theorem establishes the logical consistency of a decentralization scheme whereby terms of labour contracts are negotiated between firms and workers, under the standard control principle for the firm and majority voting by workers; whereas firms retain control over their employment and production decisions subject to the terms of their labour contracts; and consumers choose their portfolios of shares of stock and labour supply to the firms.

As noted above, when $\theta_{ij}\zeta_{ij} = 0$ (the shareholders and workers of a firm are disjoint sets of consumers), then (3.9), (3.10) and (3.11) agree with (3.6) and (3.7), so that an equilibrium for the control principle with majority voting by workers is also an equilibrium for the Pareto principle (firm by firm). And one could always substitute (3.5)–(3.7) for (3.9)–(3.11) in definitions 3.1 and 3.2 and still prove existence. These distinctions are not essential. Although the formulation adopted here strikes me (today) as the more reasonable, my views on the matter are far from rigid.

If financial markets were complete, with unique market values for all contingent claims to commodities, then an EPEC would be a competitive equilibrium in the economy with labour contracts; that is, in the economy subject to the additional constraints

$$z_s^{ij} = \frac{z_0^{ij}}{z_0^j} z_s^j \qquad s = 1, \ldots, S, \tag{3.12}$$

imposing that working times of individual workers in a given firm stand in the same ratios both in period 0 and in all states of period 1. To avoid these additional constraints, firms should offer a variety of contracts – in principle, as many different contracts as there are workers in the firm – unless workers had identical preferences.

Two extensions

Two natural extensions of the equilibrium theory covered by theorem 3.2 are worth mentioning.

First, the conditions that all labour markets clear in period 0 ($\Sigma_i \zeta_{ij} = 1 \,\forall j$) is easily relaxed to allow for *unemployment*, defined as excess supply on some market(s) for contracts. That form of unemployment (definitely involuntary from the viewpoint of individual workers) would mean that some workers do not have a contract, even though they would like to sign one at the prevailing terms. Such a situation could result from a constraint on the terms of the contracts, for instance a constraint of the form $t_s^j/z_s^j \geqslant \bar{\tau}_s$ (minimum wage). This should be accompanied by a specification of the quantity constraints ($\zeta_{ij} \leqslant \bar{\zeta}_{ij}$) on labour supply by individual consumers (for instance random rationing). There is no difficulty in relying here on the well-known theory of equilibrium with price rigidities and quantity rationing. The method of proof used for theorem 3.2 lends itself easily to that approach.[12]

Second, the equilibrium concept underlying theorem 3.2 should be extended to include incentive compatibility on the part of workers – a standard condition in implicit contracts theory. If the compensation stipulated under state s were insufficient to offset the disutility of work effort, workers would have an incentive to break their contracts by simply failing to report for work. Even though workers are not 'anonymous', the illegality of involuntary servitude would prevent firms from enforcing the contracts. The condition which we would like to introduce is that no worker i would prefer to work less in some state $s \geqslant 1$.

If all the workers employed by firm j were identical, that condition could easily be introduced in the operational form that the wage rate in any state should be at least equal to the marginal consumption–leisure trade-off there. An efficient contract would then automatically have the desired property. But workers are not identical. For instance, some get sick in state s and others in state r! One would thus like to record how many will not report for work in a given state, and to take this into account in the firm's decision. (The firm could accept the loss of output, or contract for longer hours from the remaining workers, or increase the compensation in that state to reduce absences, or combine these three adjustments.) In principle, this can be done. But the information requirements are high, and incentives for truth revelation are missing (a worker revealing that he will stay home tomorrow may not be hired today). That extension is not entirely straightforward.

Note also that an extension to several types of labour raises no new difficulty, in the present framework (where the need to forecast future spot wages does not arise).

3.4 Properties of Pareto-efficient contracts

First-order conditions

Sharper general properties of Pareto-efficient labour contracts can be spelled out under the additional assumptions of differentiability (of the production sets and of the utility functions representing consumer preferences). The derivations are given in appendix 4. Let

$$\pi_s^i = \text{def} - \left.\frac{\mathrm{d}x_0^i}{\mathrm{d}x_s^i}\right|_{u^i} = \frac{\partial u^i/\partial x_s^i}{\partial u^i/\partial x_0^i} \qquad s = 1, \ldots, S \qquad i = 1, \ldots, I \tag{3.13}$$

denote the present value for consumer i of a marginal unit of income in state s (i's personalized price, or marginal willingness to pay, for a claim contingent on state s). Let

$$\frac{\mathrm{d}x_s^i}{\mathrm{d}z_s^i} = \text{def} \left.\frac{\mathrm{d}x_s^i}{\mathrm{d}z_s^i}\right|_{u^i} = - \frac{\partial u^i/\partial z_s^i}{\partial u^i/\partial x_s^i} \qquad s = 0, 1, \ldots, S \qquad i = 1, \ldots, I \tag{3.14}$$

denote the 'reservation wage' of consumer i, either in period 0 or in period 1 state s. Let

$$\gamma_s^j = - \frac{\partial y_0^j}{\partial y_s^j} \qquad s = 1, \ldots, S \qquad j = 1, \ldots, J \tag{3.15}$$

denote the present marginal cost, for firm j, of future output in state s. Finally, let $\partial y_s^j/\partial z_s^j$, $s = 0, 1, \ldots, S$, denote the marginal product of labour in firm j, either in period 0 or in period 1, state s.

If the decision d^j is best for firm j according to the Pareto principle, then there exist positive weights μ^i, $i = 1, \ldots, I$, normalized by $\Sigma_i \, \mu^i \zeta_{ij} = \Sigma_i \, \mu^i \theta_{ij} = 1$, such that the following first-order conditions are satisfied (see appendix 4):

$$\sum_i \mu^i \theta_{ij} \pi_s^i = \sum_i \mu^i \zeta_{ij} \pi_s^i \qquad s = 1, \ldots, S \tag{3.16}$$

$$\gamma_s^j = \sum_i \mu^i \theta_{ij} \pi_s^i \qquad s = 1, \ldots, S \tag{3.17}$$

$$\frac{\partial y_0^j}{\partial z_0^j} = \sum_i \mu^i \zeta_{ij} \frac{\mathrm{d}x_0^i}{\mathrm{d}z_0^i} \tag{3.18}$$

$$\frac{\partial y_s^j}{\partial z_s^j} = \sum_i \mu^i \zeta_{ij} \pi_s^i \frac{\mathrm{d}x_s^i}{\mathrm{d}z_s^i} \Big/ \sum_i \mu^i \zeta_{ij} \pi_s^i \qquad s = 1, \ldots, S. \tag{3.19}$$

The most transparent condition is (3.18), which corresponds to (1.36). It states that the marginal product of labour in period 0 should be equal to a weighted average of the reservation wages of the workers.

The corresponding conditions for period 1 are (3.19). These could also be written as

$$\frac{\partial y_s^j}{\partial z_s^j} = \sum_i \mu^i \zeta_{ij} \frac{\mathrm{d}x_s^i}{\mathrm{d}z_s^i} + \left[\operatorname*{cov}_i \left(\pi_s^i, \frac{\mathrm{d}x_s^i}{\mathrm{d}z_s^i} \right) \Big/ \sum_i \mu^i \zeta_{ij} \pi_s^i \right]. \tag{3.20}$$

They thus take the same form as (3.18), that is equality of the marginal product of labour with the average reservation wage of workers, if and only if the personalized prices π_s^i have a zero covariance (over all consumers i, with weights $\mu^i\zeta_{ij}$) with the reservation wages. The reason why the covariance term comes in is that Pareto efficiency is defined *ex ante*, not *ex post*.[13] For instance, the reservation wages of those workers regarding state s as *impossible* are ignored in the *ex ante* condition (3.19) – although they would matter *ex post*. More generally, the tastes (reservation wage) of a given worker carry less weight when he regards a state as less likely.

For practical purposes the covariance term can probably be ignored, so that (3.19) reduces to the same standard efficiency condition for period 1 as (3.18) for period 0.

Efficient risk-sharing

Equations (3.16) state the first-order conditions on factor rewards (labour compensation and dividends) and equations (3.17) the first-order conditions on the state distribution of outputs.

In order to understand conditions (3.16), one must relate them to general properties of efficient risk-sharing – as presented, for instance, in Borch (1960) or Arrow (1970b). Let a state-dependent aggregate amount Y_s be available for division among I individuals i, each to receive a state-dependent amount y_s^i, with $\Sigma_i y_s^i = Y_s$. And let the preferences of i over such amounts be representable by the differentiable utility function $u^i(y_1^i, \ldots, y_S^i)$. With any Pareto-efficient division, one can associate a set of positive individual weights μ^i, $i = 1, \ldots, I$, such that the following conditions hold:

$$\mu^i \frac{\partial u^i}{\partial y_s^i} = \mu^h \frac{\partial u^h}{\partial y_s^h} \tag{3.21}$$

$$\frac{\partial u^i}{\partial y_s^i} \Bigg/ \frac{\partial u^i}{\partial y_r^i} = \frac{\partial u^h}{\partial y_s^h} \Bigg/ \frac{\partial u^h}{\partial y_r^h} \quad i,h, = 1, \ldots, I \quad r,s = 1, \ldots, S. \tag{3.22}$$

The weights μ^i reflect distributive options, and the whole set of Pareto-efficient divisions is generated by letting these weights range, say, over the unit simplex of R_+^I (over the set of non-negative weights μ^i satisfying $\Sigma_i \mu^i = 1$). Conditions (3.22) impose the equality of the marginal rates of substitution of all individuals among income in alternative states. These marginal rates of substitution would correspond to ratios of market prices, in an economy with a complete set of insurance markets (of markets for contingent claims). Otherwise, they correspond to 'personalized prices', or to ratios π_s^i/π_r^i in the notation above.

In the economy under consideration here, markets are not complete, but labour contracts offer the opportunity of efficient risk-sharing between the *group* of shareholders (with relative shareholdings θ_{ij}) and the *group* of workers (with relative labour supplies ζ_{ij}). The equality in (3.16) characterizes for each *s optimal mutual insurance* between the group of shareholders and the group of workers. Weighted averages of personalized prices for contingent claims are equal between the two groups. These conditions state that no further opportunities exist for mutually advantageous group insurance. As I have noted elsewhere:[14] 'It is not easy to see how this condition could be satisfied in practice, except in the simplest cases.' The two simplest cases known to me are treated later in this section.

As for (3.17), it is the standard condition for Pareto-efficient investment decisions. It is not easy to implement either, since it requires knowledge of the average personalized prices of shareholders. The condition could be stated in terms of an average over members of the control group alone, which would be much more realistic – except for the fact that a corner solution might arise from the need to obtain approval from a majority of shareholders. Still, the corner solution (γ_s^j as close to $\Sigma_i(\theta_{ij}\pi_s^i: i \in \mathscr{F}^j(\Theta))/\Sigma_i(\theta_{ij}: i \in \mathscr{F}^j(\Theta))$ as permitted by the need to obtain a majority approval) might be easier to implement than (3.17) itself.

Relation to majority voting

Before going on to consider special cases lending themselves to practical implementation, it is useful to relate these general properties of Pareto-efficient contracts to the voting equilibria of section 3.3. At such equilibria, the terms of labour contracts, namely relative working times and labour compensation, must be such that no majority of shareholders and workers would ratify a change. Upon approximating by continuous functions the distributions, over workers and shareholders respectively, of the preference parameters π_s^i and dx_s^i/dz_s^i, one should then find the first-order conditions satisfied at *median* preference parameters. (I refer to 'median preference parameters' and not to 'median voters' because the median individual is a different person in each distribution; for instance, the places of a given individual in the distributions of π_s^i and π_r^i may be widely different.) In order for these voting equilibria to induce Pareto-efficient terms for the labour contracts, the weights μ^i appearing in the first-order conditions must be such that all these conditions hold (approximately) at the median preference parameters. Denoting by $\hat{\xi}$, $\hat{\theta}$ respectively the median values for workers and shareholders, we may rewrite the relevant conditions as follows:

$$\pi_s(\hat{\xi}) = \pi_s(\hat{\theta}) \tag{3.16$'$}$$

$$\frac{\partial y_0^j}{\partial z_0^j} = \frac{dx_0}{dz_0}(\hat{\xi}) \tag{3.18$'$}$$

$$\frac{\partial y_s^j}{\partial z_s^j} = \left(\pi_s \frac{dx_s}{dz_s}\right)(\hat{\xi})/\pi_s(\hat{\xi}). \tag{3.19$'$}$$

Condition (3.19)′ would simplify to

$$\frac{\partial y_s^j}{\partial z_s^j} = \frac{dx_s}{dz_s}(\hat{\xi}) \tag{3.23}$$

if the values of π_s were equal for the worker holding the median position in the distributions of π_s^i and of $\pi_s^i(dx_s^i/dz_s^i)$ respectively – a condition close to, but still distinct from, the zero covariance condition of interest in (3.20).

The conditions (3.18)′, and (3.19)′ or (3.23), correspond to the standard result in implicit contracts theory that labour should be used efficiently (marginal value product equal to reservation wage) under all circumstances. The more interesting, and more problematic, conditions are (3.16)′, which determine the state distribution of wage payments, on the basis of perfect mutual insurance between the group of workers and the group of shareholders.

Firm-specific risks

As is well known, these conditions are easy to implement when all shareholders (or here the 'median' one) are risk neutral,[15] and all consumers agree about the probabilities of the states. Then the personalized prices of shareholders for contingent claims are all proportional to the probabilities of the states, and (3.16) implies that the average personalized prices of workers should also be proportional to the probabilities of the states. If the workers are risk averse, with state-independent preferences representable by cardinal utility functions which are separable in consumption and leisure, that is if for all i

$$u^i(x^i, z^i) = \sum_{s \geq 1} \phi_s [u^i(x_0^i, x_s^i) + u^i(z_0^i, z_s^i)] \qquad i = 1, \ldots, I, \quad (3.24)$$

then $\pi_s^i/\phi_s = \pi_1^i/\phi_1$ for all s if and only if $x_s^i = x_1^i$ for all s; that is, if and only if the consumption levels of the workers are independent of the state that obtains. This would call for labour contracts that promise a fixed income in period 1, independently of the state s and of the quantity of labour performed z_s^j. This corresponds roughly to what we observe, under full wage indexation, for salary earners (white collars), but not for wage earners (blue collars) who typically contract for fixed hourly wages and receive no bonus in case of temporary layoffs. (Conditions (3.16) would here call for a bonus equal to the difference between the fixed wage and unemployment compensation.) The existence of this distinction, and the fact that firms contract for fixed wages rather than fixed incomes, are not satisfactorily explained in the theory of implicit labour contracts. Be that as it may, we have at least one case where the conditions (3.16) would be easy to implement, since a contract promising a fixed income is easy to draw.

Risk neutrality on the part of shareholders or firms is of course an extreme assumption not tenable as such. The relevance of the discussion in the previous paragraph lies elsewhere, namely in application to specific events. There is a long tradition of distinguishing 'socially non-existent risks' from 'socially relevant risks', both in theory and in empirical analysis of stock-market data.[16] Socially non-existent risks have the property of cancelling out in the aggregate (think about the profits of two firms competing for the same sales orders) and should therefore, if marketed separately, be valued at expectation without any risk premium. Such risks are also called 'diversifiable'. In capital market theory, they are called 'firm specific' as distinct from the 'market risks' whose value entails a risk premium.

The point of relevance to our discussion here is that socially non-existent firm-specific risks should be insured away from the workers' incomes, through wage levels that remain constant across such risks. In contrast, the socially relevant market risks should be shared among all income earners or wealth holders – in proportions that vary with risk aversion, but without any group remaining exempt, according to risk-sharing theory (Borch's theorem).[17]

Compensation schemes with wages that remain constant across firm-specific contingencies are incompatible with *profit-sharing*, a system whereby workers' compensation consists of two parts – a constant part and a share of the firm's net profits.[18] That system entails some merits from the viewpoint of incentives (it might be conducive to higher labour productivity and employment than a pure wage system) but it is inefficient from the viewpoint of risk-sharing, in a stock-market economy. For smaller firms, not financed through the stock market, with equity concentrated among relatively few households, profit-sharing makes sense. If the wage bill represents the major part of value added, profit-sharing becomes important for second-best efficient risk-sharing in such privately owned firms; it should also be accompanied by a form of workers' participation in management decisions.

Market risks, the CAPM and wage indexation

Turning to socially relevant risks, there is a special case where the analysis can be made operational, namely the case covered by the Capital Asset Pricing Model (CAPM).[19] In that case, shareholders are concerned only about mean and variance of the returns to their portfolios, and consequently hold identical shares of all risky firms ($\theta_{ij} = \theta_{ik} \forall j, k$). Then the average personalized prices of shareholders for contingent claims are the same in all firms, and (3.16) implies a similar property for the personalized prices of workers. If the preferences of workers satisfy (3.24) and if the *distribution* of workers' tastes (risk aversion) is the same in all firms, then the incomes of workers should be perfectly correlated between firms. That property has a far deeper significance than I had realized at first. From the viewpoint of workers, it entails the possibility of concentrating on *economy-wide* wage negotiations, at no loss in efficiency. Firm-level contracts should only specify a general wage level – say the wage of period 0 – and hours worked (or retention probabilities) in the different states. Relative earnings w_s/w_0, $s = 1, \ldots, S$, could then be determined according to an economy-wide contract, giving content to conditions (3.16).

How would such an economy-wide contract be defined? The aim would be to satisfy conditions (3.16) between the group of all workers in the economy, and the group of all property owners. If one takes seriously the assumptions underlying the CAPM, one would be led to postulate that workers as well only care about the mean and variance of their income. In that case, an efficient allocation of risks in the whole economy would call for individual incomes (whether coming from wages or from dividends) consisting of two parts, a fixed part and a part proportional to national income, where national income equals output equals wages plus dividends.[20]

The labour contract would then stipulate an indexation formula for wages, whereby a part of the wages would be indexed on consumer prices (to define the constant part) and the other part would be indexed on nominal national income. Such a formula is almost realistic, its major drawback being that national income is not measured as rapidly, as frequently and as objectively as consumer prices. But that deficiency would be remedied to a large extent by some kind of moving average procedure.[21]

In the mean-variance portfolio models, the division of an individual's income between the fixed and the variable parts depends upon that individual's risk aversion, in relation to the average risk aversion of the market participants. Individual risk aversion is here defined by the relative measure of Arrow (1965) and Pratt (1964), namely $R_R(y) = -y[u''(y)/u'(y)]$. The relevant average risk-aversion measure is a weighted harmonic mean, with weights corresponding to income (or wealth):

$$R_R^{(H)}(y^1, \ldots, y^i, \ldots, y^I) = \Sigma_i y^i / \Sigma_i \frac{y^i}{R_R^i(y^i)}.$$

The average risk aversion $R_R^{(H)}$ is also the market risk premium, per unit of variance of aggregate wealth. Individuals who are 'more risk averse than the average', according to these definitions, hold an 'above-average' fraction of their portfolio in the safe asset; their share in the aggregate risk premium is less than their share in wealth.

Applying the same argument to labour contracts suggests that the part of individual wages indexed on consumer prices (the safe part) should be related to the risk aversion of the recipients, and should be the larger the more risk averse a worker is. Each worker could be offered the choice among all convex combinations of a reference wage fully indexed on consumer prices, and a reference wage fully indexed on nominal national income.[22] (These two reference wages would have the same market value, in terms of the market-risk premium defined on the stock exchange.) Such an arrangement would indeed be efficient, under the assumptions of the CAPM (suitably extended to encompass labour).

The model used in this chapter does not allow such fine tuning of individual wage contracts; it imposes instead that each firm should offer a single contract to all its employees. For instance, the employees could vote on the share of their common wage which is indexed on consumer prices, and the share indexed on national income. Under the assumption that the average (or median) risk aversion is approximately the same in all firms, the choice of the indexation fractions could be made at the economy-wide level. Short of relying on a voting procedure, that choice should be based on comparative estimates of the average risk aversion of workers and of the average risk aversion of property owners. We have very little solid evidence on these measures. The standard *presumption* is that workers are more risk averse than property owners, so that wage incomes should fluctuate less with national income than dividends. That presumption would be validated, for instance, if: (i) relative risk aversion were on the average the same function of wealth for workers and property owners; (ii) relative risk aversion were a decreasing function of wealth, as suggested by Arrow (1965); and (iii) property owners were on the average wealthier than workers.

The division of individual incomes into a fixed part and a part proportional to aggregate income is known as a linear sharing rule; see Wilson (1968) for a discussion of the conditions under which linear sharing rules are Pareto efficient, that is yield a solution to conditions (3.21). These conditions are quite restrictive,[23] and linear sharing rules are better viewed as a practical approximation to efficient risk-sharing than as an exact optimal solution. The empirical literature on the CAPM confirms that viewpoint, and suggests that the approximation is quite close.

I thus feel tempted to conclude this section with the suggestion that efficient labour contracts could be reasonably well approximated through a new indexation formula, whereby wages might be indexed on consumer prices up to some base amount and on nominal national income beyond that base amount. That formula would be applied in all cases where the owners of the firm could be presumed to hold market portfolios. The main exceptions to that presumption would seem to concern privately owned firms, where a form of profit-sharing between the capital owners and the workers would make sense, but would then justify workers' participation in decision-making. In both cases, the wages under consideration should be understood per period, not per hour - calling for special bonuses on behalf of temporarily laid-off workers.

Notes

1 Similarly, z_0^j could be split into a part devoted to investment and a part devoted to current production.

2 As a simple example, let output y_s^j in period 1, state s, be proportional to a function of capital investment in period 0, say k^j, and of labour input z_s^j; the factor of proportionality, say b_s^j, reflects the technological choice made in period 0 (composition and direction of investment). Then

$$y_s^j = b_s^j f_s^j(k^j, z_s^j) \qquad s = 1, \ldots, S \qquad (k^j, b_1^j, \ldots, b_S^j) \in B^j$$

where B^j describes the set of technological choices open to the firm. More generally, one could write

$$y_s^j = f_s^j(k^j, z_s^j, b^j) \qquad s = 1, \ldots, S \qquad (k^j, b^j) \in B^j \subset R^{S+1}$$

where b^j is a vector of 'characteristics' of the investment. Or one could consider a finite set of investment projects indexed $a = 1, \ldots, A$ and write

$$y_s^j = f_s^j(k_1^j, \ldots, k_a^j, \ldots, k_A^j, z_s^j) \qquad s = 1, \ldots, S \qquad k^j = \sum_a k_a^j$$

where k_a^j denotes the amount invested in project a.

3 See for example, Drèze (1979, sections 3 and 4) for an informal presentation of the rationale of that theory; and the survey papers listed in note 9 of chapter 2 in this book.

4 In the literature, the second possibility is often ignored by assuming that all workers are identical; it is retained, for instance, by Hart (1983).

5 In so far as future labour inputs are concerned, this is also the more relevant case when the organization of work requires coordination of working schedules.

6 In chapter 1, had there been a single type of labour, we could have defined $\zeta_{ij} = z^{ij}/z^j$. Alternatively, if labour time is fixed, and all workers hold a single full-time job, $\zeta_{ij} = 1/z^j$, where z^j is the number of employees in firm j.

7 More realistically that possibility should be reserved for special categories of workers, such as auditors, window-cleaners, lawyers and gardeners.

8 For instance Holmström (1983).

9 *Strict* convexity of preferences is *not* preserved, since the decisions of the

firms may imply linearly dependent production plans or labour contracts.

10 An example showing how imperfections of the stock market may hurt workers (by resulting in lower wages) is given in section 4.2.

11 If (3.10) were stated in terms of weak preferences ($\succsim_i$ instead of $\succ_i$), then definition 3.1 would be a special case of definition 3.2, and would not need to be listed separately in the equilibrium definition to follow.

12 See Greenberg and Müller (1979), extending Drèze (1975).

13 For the relevance of that distinction, see for example Drèze (1971) or Guesnerie and de Montbrial (1974).

14 See Drèze (1976, p. 1135).

15 With complete markets, it would suffice that *some* shareholders be risk neutral. Arbitrage conditions on asset markets would then lead to risk-trading at no risk premium. With incomplete markets, however, the risk-averse shareholders do not have the opportunity to equate their marginal rates of substitution with probabilities, through trading with the risk-neutral shareholders.

16 See for example Allais (1953) on the theoretical side, or Modigliani and Pogue (1974) on the empirical side.

17 See conditions (3.21) and (3.22).

18 There are two variants of profit-sharing, one where the profit share of each worker is predetermined, and another (mostly considered by Weitzman 1984) where the aggregate profit share of labour is predetermined and individual shares are allowed to depend *ex post* upon the hiring policy of the firm. That distinction is not relevant to the discussion in the text.

19 See for example Mossin (1977) or Modigliani and Pogue (1974).

20 In a two-period model, the second-period national income is also the national wealth, as of the beginning of the second period; in multiperiod models, the relevant concept is wealth, for which income may (or may not) serve as a good proxy.

21 A similar suggestion already appears in Drèze (1979, section 9(a)).

22 These wage options may be compared with the capitalization options offered to US academics by their pension fund (TIAA), which gives them the choice among convex combinations of a reference portfolio of bonds and a reference portfolio of stocks.

23 Either one places undesirable restrictions (like normality) on the probability distribution of aggregate income, or one requires that the preferences of all individuals be representable by utility functions of the same functional form (quadratic, exponential, logarithmic or identical power functions). In addition, all individuals must agree about the probabilities of the states.

CHAPTER 4

Labour Management versus Labour Contracts under Incomplete Capital Markets

4.1 Financing labour-managed firms under incomplete markets

Internal financing

The model used in section 3.2 lends itself easily to a labour-management reinterpretation. This will be developed in three steps, namely: internal financing, bond financing and equity financing.

Internal financing means that the investment needs of every firm must be met from the resources and savings of the members, that is of the workers in the firm. In the model of chapter 3, this condition can be imposed in either one of two ways; the first is more restrictive but in a sense purer; the second is somewhat less restrictive but more hybrid.

The 'purer' specification takes the simple form

$$\theta_{ij} = \zeta_{ij} \qquad \forall\, i,j. \tag{4.1}$$

That is, the workers in the firm are also the shareholders, in the same proportions.[1] Under this specification, workers would share the value added, both in period 0 and in period 1 under all states, in proportion to their labour contributions. We would still need to introduce the rents r^j of chapter 1 for access to the initial productive assets. Generality suggests that rents be paid partly in period 0, say r^j_0, and partly in period 1, r^j_1. Rights to shares in these rents would still be apportioned independently of membership in the firms – say in given proportions $\bar{\theta}_{ij}$. The vector defining value added in firm j would thus be

$$(y_0^j - r_0^j, y_1^j - r_1^j, \ldots, y_s^j - r_1^j, \ldots, y_S^j - r_1^j) = \text{def } y^j - r^j.$$

Each consumer would now choose a vector ζ_i of membership fractions in the firms (typically but not necessarily with $\zeta_{ij} > 0$ for a single j), leading to a consumption and labour plan defined by:

$$z^i = \sum_j \zeta_{ij} z^j \tag{4.2}$$

$$x_0^i = w_0^i + \sum_j \bar{\theta}_{ij} r_0^j + \sum_j \zeta_{ij}(y_0^j - r_0^j) \tag{4.3}$$

$$x_s^i = w_s^i + \sum_j \bar{\theta}_{ij} r_1^j + \sum_j \zeta_{ij}(y_s^j - r_1^j) \qquad s = 1, \ldots, S. \tag{4.4}$$

This is a simplified and more constrained version of the economy considered in section 3.2. The simplification comes from the fact that the division of value added between capital and labour no longer needs to be specified. The additional constraints, which also entail the simplification, were introduced in (4.1).

It follows immediately that the set of allocations attainable in this economy forms a *proper subset* of those attainable in the earlier formulation. The restrictive nature of conditions (4.1) has two aspects: a savings aspect and a risk-sharing aspect.

The *savings* aspect is well known, and has been stressed in the literature as a major explanation for the limited development of labour-managed firms within capitalist economies.[2] On the one hand, it is difficult to see how the handful of workers operating a supertanker, a jumbo jet or an oil refinery would ever save up the huge capital required to procure their working equipment. On the other hand, it has been noted that workers operating an ongoing capital-intensive concern would shy away from investments outlasting their own working life. On both counts, underinvestment would result, and labour-managed firms would find themselves confined to the more labour-intensive, low-investment sectors of the economy. For instance, such firms could operate fishing boats, taxis or filling stations – a picture that corresponds well to experience, with a few notable exceptions.

The *risk-sharing* aspect is stated concisely but forcefully by Meade (1972, p. 426):

> While property owners can spread their risks by putting small bits of their property into a large number of concerns, a worker cannot put small bits of his effort into a large number of different jobs. This presumably is a main reason why we find risk-bearing capital hiring labour rather than risk-bearing labour hiring

> capital. Moreover, since labour cannot spread its risks, we are likely to find cooperative structures only in lines of activity in which the risk is not too great, and this means in lines of activity in which two conditions are fulfilled: first, the risk of fluctuations in the demand for the product must not be too great; and secondly, the activity must be labour intensive, in which the surplus accruing to labour does not constitute a small difference between two large quantities, the revenues from the sale of the product and the hire of capital plus the purchase of raw materials.[3]

This line of reasoning is quite convincing and is borne out by casual observation. The risks per head supported by the crew of a supertanker or a jumbo jet, if the vessel or craft laid idle due to insufficient demand but still required maintenance and amortization, is simply too much for the workers to bear. Risk diversification by shareholders protecting the workers through efficient labour contracts seems indispensable for that kind of activity.

A somewhat less restrictive form of conditions (4.1) is obtained if we write instead

$$\zeta_{ij} = 0 \Rightarrow \theta_{ij} = 0 \qquad \forall\, i,j. \tag{4.5}$$

This formulation still imposes that all shares of stock be held by the workers, but allows them to contribute labour and capital in different proportions. The precise formulation (4.5) is not quite operational, because it allows a consumer to own a firm fully on the basis of an arbitrarily small contribution to its labour inputs. A more operational constraint would be, say:

$$\underline{k}\,\zeta_{ij} \leqslant \theta_{ij} \leqslant \bar{k}\zeta_{ij} \qquad \forall\, i,j. \tag{4.6}$$

The special case (4.1) corresponds to $\underline{k} = \bar{k} = 1$. For values of $\underline{k}$ and $\bar{k}$ that do not diverge too much from unity, all the problems associated with (4.1) remain acute. If on the contrary $\underline{k}$ and $\bar{k}$ diverge sufficiently to permit bypassing these problems, we are then faced with a situation where the firm consists of two types of members: one type supplies mostly labour (and a token amount of capital), and the other type supplies mostly capital (and a token amount of labour).[4] Some rules about the division of value added and the apportionment of control rights must be devised, and for all practical purposes we are in a situation of equity financing; or at any rate in a situation more conveniently discussed under the heading of equity financing.

Bond financing

The form of external financing most easily reconciled with labour management is often alleged to be bond financing. Bond holders, who bear no risks, are not involved in the firm's management, which may thus remain vested with the workers; in contrast equity holders, who bear risks, typically receive control rights over management, thereby encroaching upon the prerogatives of workers.

Formally, this case is already covered by (4.2)–(4.4), if we let r_0^j become negative to represent the loan, and if we denote the repayment by r_1^j (both figures being possibly adjusted for a rent on initial assets).

It should be intuitively clear that bond financing provides an answer to the savings problem raised above, but not to the risk-sharing problem. The crew of a supertanker could possibly borrow the capital needed to acquire the ship, but bonds call for a fixed repayment, independently of the state, so that the borrowers would inevitably go bankrupt in bad states. In the words of Meade, value added would constitute the highly risky difference between the uncertain returns from operating the tanker and the sizeable fixed commitment to the bond holders. Again, that risk is simply too much for the workers to bear (assuming that willing lenders could be found).

Equity financing

We are thus led to consider equity financing as the *only* form of external financing presenting the labour-managed firms with adequate opportunities for risk-sharing; where equity financing means raising investment capital, not against promise of a fixed repayment, but against promise of a *state-dependent* repayment.

Write $e^j = (e_0^j, e_1^j, \ldots, e_S^j)$ in $R_- \times R_+^S$ for the initial capital investment e_0^j and state-dependent repayments e_s^j to capital (equity) owners. In the case of a labour-managed firm run by the workers, the repayment to capital owners is not a residual claim; it must be stipulated contractually, say in an 'equity contract'.[5] A decision d^j for the labour-managed firm j will thus consist of a production plan $(y^j, z^j) \in Y^j$ and an equity contract e^j in $R_- \times R_+^S$. Such a decision entails a *vector* of aggregate net value added $v^j = (v_0^j, v_1^j, \ldots, v_S^j)$, where

$$v_s^j = y_s^j - r_s^j - e_s^j \qquad s = 0, 1, \ldots, S. \tag{4.7}$$

To facilitate comparisons without loss of generality, let me assume that $r_1^j = r_2^j = \ldots = r_S^j = 0$ (all rents are paid in period 0, possibly by means of equity capital). Still writing θ_{ij} for the share of consumer i in the equity capital of firm j, and $\bar{\theta}_{ij}$ for i's share in the rent levied on firm j, I will let each consumer choose a vector θ_i of equity shares, and a vector ζ_i of labour shares. The resulting consumption and labour plan is defined by:

$$z^i = \sum_j \zeta_{ij} z^j \tag{4.8}$$

$$x_0^i = w_0^i + \sum_j \bar{\theta}_{ij} r_0^j + \sum_j \zeta_{ij} v_0^j + \sum_j \theta_{ij}(y_0^j - v_0^j - r_0^j) \tag{4.9}$$

$$x_s^i = w_s^i + \sum_j \zeta_{ij} v_s^j + \sum_j \theta_{ij}(y_s^j - v_s^j) \qquad s = 1, \ldots, S \tag{4.10}$$

where use has been made of (4.7) to express e_s^j in (4.9) and (4.10) in terms of the remaining variables y_s^j, v_s^j and r_s^j. The substitution has been made so as to bring out the *formal identity* between (4.8)–(4.10) and (3.2)–(3.4). The equity contract e^j has replaced the labour contract (z^j, t^j) to define the division between capital and labour of the gross value added associated with the production plan (y^j, z^j); and the rent r^j has replaced the stock price p_j. Clearly, the set of allocations attainable through labour contracts in the stock-market economy of section 3.2 coincides with the set of allocations attainable through equity contracts in the labour-managed economy of this section.[6]

This conclusion is in the nature of an *accounting identity*. Given (y^j, z^j), if we set $r_0^j \equiv p_j$, then to any labour contract (z^j, t^j) there corresponds an equity contract e^j, defined uniquely through (4.7) by setting there $v_s^j = t_s^j$, $s = 0, 1, \ldots, S$; and conversely. Furthermore, when defining attainable allocations, we may choose $p \in R_+^J$ and $r_0 \in R_+^J$ freely – subject possibly to the common restriction $p_j = r_0^j = 0$ whenever Y^j corresponds to freely replicable technological knowledge.

4.2 Labour contracts versus equity contracts

Labour-management equilibria with equity contracts

The next step should obviously consist in defining an equilibrium concept for equity-financed labour-managed firms. Not surprisingly, value added per unit of labour is no longer a well-defined criterion, because value added v^j is a *vector* in R^{S+1} and not a scalar. In the same way that profit maximization is ill defined under incomplete markets, so is maximization of value added per unit of labour. And in the same way that we were led in chapter 2 to consider aggregation of shareholders' preferences, so we are now led to consider aggregation of workers' preferences. The two problems are almost identical, the only difference being that workers are here concerned with pairs of vectors (z^j, v^j) defining their labour inputs and labour incomes, whereas shareholders were only concerned with vectors of property incomes. But the need to aggregate heterogeneous preferences over individuals raises the same logical issue in both cases. (Practical issues may still be quite different: workers are much closer to each other than shareholders; shareholders face lower transaction costs in reshuffling their portfolios than workers do in changing jobs; and so on.)

Also, in the same way that it was in the interest of shareholders to look for efficient labour contracts (for otherwise they could retain the same labour services at less cost to themselves), so it is now in the interest of workers to look for efficient equity contracts. Efficient equity contracts must have the property that there exists no alternative contract more attractive to all concerned; that is, they must satisfy the Pareto principle for the labour-managed firm.

These simple ideas, which flow naturally from the statement of the problem, seem acceptable enough.[7] Still, some qualifications are mentioned later in this section.

It is a routine task to define a *labour-management equilibrium with equity contracts* (LMEC) to consist of a rent vector $r \in R^J_+$, a set of decisions $d^j, j = 1, \ldots, J$, and a set of portfolios $(\theta_i, \zeta_i), i = 1, \ldots, I$, $1 \geqslant \theta_{ij} \geqslant 0, 1 \geqslant \zeta_{ij} \geqslant 0$; in short, a quadruple (r,d,Θ,Z) such that

(i) For each i, (θ_i, ζ_i) induces via (4.8)–(4.10) a consumption and labour plan $(x^i, z^i) \in C^i$, and there exists no alternative portfolio $(\hat{\theta}_i, \hat{\zeta}_i)$ such that the induced $(\hat{x}^i, \hat{z}^i)$ belongs to C^i with $(\hat{x}^i, \hat{z}^i) >_i (x^i, z^i)$.

(ii) For each j, $\Sigma_i \theta_{ij} = 1$ and $\Sigma_i \zeta_{ij} = 1$.

(iii) For each j, $d^j = (y^j, z^j, e^j) \in D^j = Y^j \times R_- \times R^S_+$, and the decision d^j is best for firm j over D^j at (r,d,Θ,Z).

Under a given portfolio (θ_i, ζ_i) and given the decisions d^k in all firms $k \neq j$, consumer i will have an ordering on the decisions d^j of firm j defined by

$$\hat{d}^j >_i d^j \quad \text{if and only if} \quad (\hat{x}^i, \hat{z}^i) >_i (x^i, z^i) \tag{4.11}$$

where

$$\hat{x}^i = x^i + \theta_{ij}(\hat{y}^j - \hat{v}^j - y^j + v^j) + \zeta_{ij}(\hat{v}^j - v^j) \tag{4.12}$$

$$\hat{z}^i = z^i + \zeta_{ij}(\hat{z}^j - z^j). \tag{4.13}$$

Definition 2.1″ (Pareto principle with equity contracts)

(i) $\hat{d}^j$ is better for j than d^j at (r,d,Θ,Z) if and only if $\hat{d}^j >_i d^j$ according to (4.11)–(4.13) for all i with $\theta_{ij} + \zeta_{ij} > 0$.
(ii) d^j is best for j over D^j at (r,d,Θ,Z) if and only if D^j does not contain any $\hat{d}^j$ better than d^j according to (i).

Proposition 4.1

The sets of allocations that can be sustained as labour-management equilibria with Pareto-efficient equity contracts (as per definition 2.1″) and as equilibria of production, exchange and Pareto-efficient labour contracts (as per definition 2.1′) are identical.

Proof

If (r,d,Θ,Z) is a labour-management equilibrium for definition 2.1″, let $p = r$, $t^j = v^j$, $j = 1, \ldots, J$. Then (p,d,Θ,Z) is an EPEC for definition 2.1′. Indeed, the allocation is attainable, and the equilibrium conditions are identical. The same reasoning applies to the converse implication. □

This proposition is analogous to corollary 1.1. As was noted in section 2.1, the proposition is weaker and almost definitional, once it has been observed that labour contracts and equity contracts are related by the accounting identity (4.7). Still, it brings out the relationship of the rents r_0^j to stock prices p_j, a relationship that was not entirely obvious *a priori* (even though it is transparent *ex post*). The weakness of the proposition is basically the weakness of an equilibrium concept that relies on the Pareto principle alone to characterize firm behaviour. More definite behavioural assumptions would be needed for sharper conclusions. Yet the properties of Pareto-efficient contracts discussed in section 3.4 become applicable to labour-management equilibria as well.

I am not aware of any convincing analysis of decision criteria for labour-managed firms, with heterogeneous members, in a world of uncertainty with incomplete markets. Majority voting, although frequently mentioned, is not a satisfactory decision procedure, in view of the Condorcet paradox (intransitivity).

The idea of a control group, as introduced in chapter 2, is less appealing for decisions by workers than for decisions by shareholders. On the one hand, workers are more intimately concerned than shareholders, and thus less likely to surrender control to a minority group. On the other hand, the very idea of labour management calls for democratic decision procedures, a feature not shared by capitalism with absentee ownership. Still, one could in principle extend the analysis of chapter 3 to labour management.

Note also that a labour-managed firm operating efficiently in a framework like that of the present chapter would not maximize value added per worker *ex post* in the second period. Operating there with a fixed membership, it would rather choose its labour inputs (hours worked) so as to equate the marginal value product of labour to the average (median) reservation wage of the members, according to conditions (3.19) and (3.20). The terms of the equity contract should be such as to generate proper incentives to that effect. The resulting vector of value added per worker, both in period 0 and in every state s of period 1, would still determine initial membership, but not working hours in every state.

Labour management and labour contracts

Weak as it may be, proposition 4.1 has some very useful implications. They concern first the role of labour contracts, and of labour contracts theory, in models of labour-managed economies. They concern also the reconciliation of productive efficiency and risk-sharing under alternative forms of organization.

A surprising implication of proposition 4.1 is that a labour-managed firm could *indifferently* negotiate with the suppliers of its capital an equity contract (specifying the dividends under every state) or a labour contract (specifying a labour input and a wage bill under every state). The real consequences of both contracts would be identical for both parties, with only the words used to describe these consequences differing as between the two documents. If both parties trusted each other fully and were unconcerned about terminology, they might agree to use the simpler terms, whichever these may be. If the real consequences were more conveniently described in terms of state-contingent labour inputs and wage bills than in terms of dividends, we might observe the paradox of a labour-managed firm signing a labour contract with its shareholders!

Thus, consider again the special case described at the end of section 3.4. In that case, an efficient contract called for real labour incomes consisting of two parts: a lump-sum part; and a variable part, linked to national income but unrelated to firm-specific risks. The efficient contract also called for working hours in every state equating the marginal product of labour to its opportunity cost. Such a contract is relatively easy to stipulate. The income part simply requires agreement on a measure of national income and an indexing formula. And one could even generate automatically the desired working time, by simply stipulating that the value of a worker's marginal product should be subtracted from the wage bill if he or she did not report to work. Such a labour contract would be perfectly consistent with the spirit of labour management. In addition, it would be much easier to draw than the corresponding equity contract, which would need to stipulate the level of dividends under each state – a formidable task under most circumstances, unless the wage bill were used (albeit implicitly) to define the dividends.[8]

Note that the difficulty of drawing efficient equity contracts is more severe for firm-specific diversifiable risks than for socially relevant market risks. The latter could be handled by linking dividends to national income. But the former would need to be spelled out in details specific to the firm, and that is much more difficult. The attractiveness of the simple labour contract under discussion is that it transfers conveniently the firm-specific risks to a market pool, whilst drawing the workers into the pool to share efficiently the market risks. The ease with which a labour contract performs these twin functions may be viewed as an indirect confirmation of the arguments to the effect that labour-managed firms should be equity financed, in general.

Of course, there remains an important difference between the two formulations, namely how they affect incentives. Under the equity contracts, workers are committed to pay certain levels of dividends, and their own incomes in all states are directly affected by deviations from the productivity levels conditional on which these dividends were stipulated. Under the labour contract formulation, these deviations affect dividends instead. Hence, incentives to achieve adequate labour productivity[9] are more directly implied by the equity contract than by the labour contract.[10] Note however that productivity fluctuations may be due to causes other than working effort (quality of inputs, performance of equipment, weather, behaviour of customers and so on). These causes may be difficult to enumerate (together with their impact on value added) in the equity contract, in which case the equity contract would fail to imply the degree of labour income stability corresponding to efficient risk-sharing.

We have just entered the intriguing area of observability of states and asymmetries of information, which has inspired some interesting contributions to the theory of implicit labour contracts.[11] These complications, which play an important role in practical decisions about the preferred formulation of contracts or even about the preferred mode of organization, are not covered here. In stressing the fact that efficient labour contracts are typically easier to draw than efficient equity contracts, I am addressing a more sophisticated issue than the risk-diversification issue stressed by Meade (who does not consider the possibility of equity financing for labour-managed firms), but perhaps a less sophisticated issue than those considered in the literature on incentives, asymmetries of information and so on. Of course, all these issues are simultaneously relevant.

The specific point which I am making here is that labour contracts may provide the more natural vehicle for defining labour–capital relationships *also in the case of labour-managed firms*, when the risk-sharing aspect is recognized. And there are known instances of partnerships organized in precisely that way, with an autonomous manager drawing a fixed salary (and presumably finding an incentive to maximize the residual profit in his expectation to negotiate a rise or to extend the partnership on terms reflecting his productivity).

A dual observation is that participation in actual decision-making may not be required for safeguarding the interests of workers, if there is scope for negotiating comprehensive labour contracts. In other words, labour contracts offer an *alternative* to participatory decision-making.[12] Drawing upon the lessons of chapter 1, one may even speculate about the prospects for combining, in capitalist firms, efficient labour contracts with (possibly decentralized) labour-managed decisions about working conditions.

Labour contracts versus equity contracts

Proposition 4.1 implies that all the developments in the theory of efficient labour contracts are of direct relevance to the theory of labour-managed economies; for the results apply automatically to efficient equity contracts, as Miyazaki and Neary (1983) have already noted.

As an illustration of this point, I wish to correct some erroneous statements regarding the reconciliation of productive efficiency and risk-sharing, which I made a few years ago before becoming acquainted with the implicit contracts literature. In Drèze (1976, pp. 1136–7), I discussed the first-order conditions for Pareto-efficient decisions by a firm, and in particular the conditions (3.19) defining levels of labour inputs. I commented as follows:

> These natural conditions are not compatible with decentralized incentives when efficient rules for the division of output are adopted. When labour hires capital it would not be in the interest of workers to equate their marginal rate of substitution between work and income to the marginal product of their labour unless that marginal product accrued entirely to them. But efficient risk-bearing typically requires another division. When capital hires labour, the wage rates required for efficient risk-bearing are not equal, *ex post*, to the marginal product of labour. Wages that serve a function of income insurance cannot simultaneously measure labour productivity. Hence these wages do not sustain, *ex post*, the efficient allocations as decentralized competitive equilibria.[13]

These remarks, which may be summed up as stating that decisions which are Pareto efficient *ex ante* fail to be 'incentive compatible' *ex post*, lose relevance in a 'contracts' framework. Thus workers may find it in their interest to equate their reservation wage to the marginal product of their labour in state s, even though their share in the marginal value added there is less than 100 per cent, because the additional dividend to capital owners in state s is matched under the terms of the equity contract by more labour income in some other state r. The superiority of the contract over spot transactions under each state is precisely that it permits this type of trade-off, thereby enabling the two groups (capital owners and workers) to engage in mutual insurance. Similarly, firms will be willing to pay wages exceeding the marginal product of labour in some states, if the contract stipulates wages lower than that marginal product in other states (or in period 0). *If* the contracts themselves are either enforceable or incentive compatible, the difficulties mentioned in the above quotation are bypassed.

All these comments contribute to an identification of the conditions under which either form of organization – labour contracts or equity contracts – is more likely to emerge. Convenience in drawing up the contracts has been stressed, and has been linked to observability of the states. Monitoring contracts is another important aspect, already recognized in the early literature on sharecropping.[14] Monitoring by shareholders under labour management concerns mostly managerial abilities, capital maintenance and work effort. Under capitalism, monitoring by labour also concerns managerial abilities and dividends policy, since the workers are concerned about the occurrence of 'bad states' and about bankruptcy.[15]

When efficient contracts are too difficult to draw in either form, some simple second-best solution will emerge. This may take the form of fixed wage contracts with redundancy notice and/or severance pay; or it may take the form of bond financing for labour-managed firms. We would expect the former solution to prevail whenever the risk-sharing preoccupation dominates, and the latter to become more likely when efficiency in using labour is crucial. Thus operating a supertanker is best left to capitalist firms hiring sailors. But fishing is more naturally organized on a labour-managed basis, because the decisions whether or not to continue fishing under adverse, possibly hazardous or unproductive conditions are best left to the fishermen out at sea and are difficult to stipulate in a contract.

By way of conclusion to this chapter, I still wish to mention that workers signing either a labour contract or an equity contract remain concerned with the efficiency of the risk-sharing arrangements among shareholders, and/or the definitions of control groups.

A simple example should make this point clear. Consider an economy with two firms, two states, two resource owners supplying working capital but no labour, and a continuum of workers supplying their labour to a single firm each. All consumers have state-independent endowments – say unity. The production set of firm j is defined by $y_1^j = z_1^j$, $y_2^j = 0$; that of firm k by $y_1^k = 0$, $y_2^k = z_2^k$. The preferences of workers are defined by $u(x_1, x_2, z_1, z_2) = \min(x_1, x_2) - \alpha \max(z_1^2, z_2^2)$ (infinite risk aversion); the preferences of resource owners are defined by $u(x_1,x_2) = 2x_1^{1/2} + 2x_2^{1/2}$. It follows that all efficient contracts must stipulate the same labour income in both states. Equilibrium will require a wage level l common to both firms and such that labour supply equals labour demand. A worker will thus supply a quantity of labour which maximizes $1 + lz - \alpha z^2$, namely $z = l/2\alpha$. Let α and the number (measure) of workers be such that aggregate labour supply is equal to $2l$.

If each resource owner holds a portfolio consisting of 50 per cent of both firms, and if both firms employ the same number of workers z (as required for overall efficiency), then the utility of a resource owner will be

$$2[1 + \tfrac{1}{2}z(1-l) - \tfrac{1}{2}zl]^{1/2} + 2[1 - \tfrac{1}{2}zl + \tfrac{1}{2}z(1-l)]^{1/2} = 4[1 + \tfrac{1}{2}z(1-2l)]^{1/2}.$$

Both shareholders will insist on hiring more labour if $l < 1/2$, less labour if $l > 1/2$, so that the only equilibrium is reached at $l = 1/2$, $z = 1$.

Suppose now that each resource owner holds a fixed portfolio consisting of 100 per cent of a single firm. His utility is then

$$2[1 + z(1-l)]^{1/2} + 2(1-zl)^{1/2}.$$

Maximizing this expression with respect to z leads to a labour demand

$$z = \frac{1-zl}{l(1-l)}.$$

Equilibrium requires $z = l$, so that aggregate labour demand $2z$ is equal to aggregate supply $2l$. One then verifies numerically that the equilibrium wage is now less than 1/2, so that all workers are worse off.

Notes

1 With a single type of labour, the condition is straightforward; with different types of labour, it might become $\theta_{ij} = \Sigma_l a_{jl} z_l^{ij} / \Sigma_{hl} a_{jl} z_l^{hj}$.

2 See, for instance, Jensen and Meckling (1979), Furubotn and Pejovich (1973), Vanek (1971) or Defourny (1982) for a survey and additional references.

3 See also Meade (1982, section IX–4).

4 In order to bypass the difficulty for a worker of putting small bits of his effort into a large number of different jobs, the labour input of a consumer

holding a diversified portfolio should indeed be reduced to little more than attending shareholders meetings.

5 Some amount of bond financing may of course be implicit in an equity contract, if $e_s^j > 0$ for all $s = 1, \ldots, S$.

6 To be precise, the equivalence holds if the limited liability condition (3.1) is imposed on the stock-market economy; or alternatively if the equity contract is not restricted to limited liability and is allowed to stipulate $e_s^j < 0$ in some states.

7 As already mentioned in chapter 2, similar ideas are already present in the partial equilibrium analysis of Miyazaki and Neary (1983).

8 Two simple examples may help. A firm producing electricity will find it easier to stipulate a wage bill than a dividend level, unless dividends were *defined* as value added minus labour's share. A firm operating a filling station on a rigid schedule will similarly stipulate either a wage bill, or dividends defined as say, so many cents per gallon minus fixed cost minus labour's share. The point made in the text is that labour's share is given by a simple operational formula in the special case of section 3.4.

9 Neither too low, nor so high as to demand efforts which are inadequately remunerated at the margin.

10 More directly, because longer-run considerations (renewing the contract on favourable terms) may provide the proper incentives in both cases.

11 See for example Geanakoplos and Ito (1982) or Grossman and Hart (1983).

12 Returning to the example given in section 2.1, the adequate compensation of the worker with specialized skills in case of failure would be stipulated in an efficient labour contract.

13 That statement has been criticized by Jensen and Meckling (1979) as committing the 'Nirvana fallacy' of contrasting an ideal labour-managed system with a real-world capitalist alternative. I thought that I was clearly comparing two ideal systems – which might be termed a 'Nirvana^2 fallacy'!

14 See for example, the seminal paper by Stiglitz (1974), or the survey by Newbery and Stiglitz (1979).

15 On the very day of checking this chapter (8 April 1988), I heard on the radio that the employees of a firm in Liège, Belgium, were going on strike to oppose a dividend policy viewed by them as apt to restrict the future investment potential of the firm.

CHAPTER 5

Some Macroeconomic Aspects, and Conclusions

5.1 Provisional conclusions

So far, I have considered the relationship between labour and capital at the *firm* level, while taking into account some implications of market clearing. Two main conclusions stand out. In a world of complete markets with labour mobility, no specific gains should be expected, in equilibrium, from action by labour at the firm level: labour-management equilibria correspond to competitive (wage) equilibria. In a more realistic world of uncertainty with incomplete markets, efficient risk-sharing between capital owners (holding diversified portfolios) and workers (unable to protect their human capital through diversification) is not organized by the market and requires instead sophisticated *contractual* arrangements.

In the capitalist system, labour contracts (explicit or implicit) are the institutional support of such arrangements. Under labour management, equity contracts would be needed to the same end, but do not seem to be in systematic use, either in Yugoslavia or in capitalist countries.

Uncertainty is the standard instance of incomplete markets, but it is by no means the only one. In so far as labour services are concerned, working schedules and working conditions are other significant instances.[1] As indicated already in chapter 1, these are in the nature of public goods – on a par with the investment decisions considered in chapters 2–4. These decisions do not seem to be fully guided by market-clearing prices, and require some form of collective decision-making at the firm level.

In so far as working conditions are concerned, labour management seems to be a natural answer. Experience suggests that partnerships are most common in situations where working conditions are an important parameter, and capital requirements are low. In so far as uncertainty is concerned, capital markets are the natural answer, because they allow for efficient risk-sharing through portfolio diversification. The standard argument, to the effect that workers are unable to bear themselves the risks of capital-intensive ventures, is a valid one. But it does not preclude equity financing of labour-managed firms. To explain why that form of organization is seldom practised, I think that one must invoke the relative difficulty of stipulating and monitoring efficient equity contracts, for labour-managed firms, in a world of uncertainty and incomplete markets. In comparison, efficient labour contracts are easier to draw. Also, the more developed are capital markets, the easier it becomes to write down efficient labour contracts.[2] In the interesting case where all firm-specific risks are diversified away through capital markets, efficient labour contracts would simply link labour incomes to national income, to a first approximation. Drawing instead an efficient equity contract would be a very difficult task, and monitoring the contract would either be very cumbersome or be equivalent to restoring indirectly a 'capital hires labour' situation.

Efficient labour contracts transfer to workers the benefits of efficient risk-sharing on capital markets. It was noted in chapter 3 that prevailing labour contracts seem to be less than fully efficient in that respect. That remark suggests scope for improvement, about which more later; it also casts additional doubts on the practical feasibility of implementing efficient equity contracts.

These considerations go a long way towards explaining why labour management remains exceptional in industrial societies, in spite of its moral appeal and of the fact (theoretically documented in chapter 1) that it could easily coexist with salaried employment. But the analysis at the firm level must still be extended on two counts, of a more macroeconomic nature.

5.2 A static macroeconomic aspect

Labour's comparative advantage

It was noted in chapter 3 that efficient capital markets would, as a first approximation (at the level of approximation embodied in the capital asset pricing model), result in individual portfolios combining a safe asset with identical tiny shares of all firms. As a consequence, all firms would have the same shareholders, or at any rate shareholders with similar preferences. If risk preferences of workers in different firms were also similar, it would then follow that, to a first approximation, efficient labour contracts imply labour incomes that are perfectly correlated across firms. In other words, a single labour contract drawn for the whole economy would come close to achieving overall efficiency; negotiations over the terms of labour contracts could become centralized at the economy-wide level, at a substantial saving of time and effort in conducting the negotiations. The counterpart for that property, in so far as the equity contracts of labour-managed firms are concerned, is that efficient contracts could be based on a stipulation of labour incomes geared to a national formula, with the rest of value added going to capital. These equity contracts would thus be indistinguishable from labour contracts.

Of course, the statements just made only hold as a first approximation. Actual capital markets do not exactly operate as predicted by the CAPM. Not all firms are financed through shares traded on the stock exchange. Individual firms, including those quoted on the stock exchange, are controlled by managers and directors, whose decisions need not fully reflect shareholder preferences. Fear of bankruptcy, which typically generates significant transaction costs, leads to aversion *vis-à-vis* individual (diversifiable) risks and to greater risk aversion at the firm level than at the market level. As noted earlier, the employees of individual firms may be particularly concerned with specific risks (because their human capital is specialized). Employees of different firms may also display different degrees of risk aversion, due for instance to self-selection or to demographic characteristics.[3] But all this being said, it remains true that negotiating the terms of labour contracts at the economy-wide level is apt to capture most of the benefits associated with efficient risk-sharing, and to avoid most of the transaction costs associated with decentralized negotiations at the firm level.

The significance of that remark is enhanced by the fact that, to a large extent, labour organizations derive their strength from their ability to operate across firms, at the level of a craft, of an industrial sector or even of the whole economy. At these levels, labour unions are in a much better position to exert an influence on the terms of the labour contracts of capitalist firms than on the terms of the equity contracts of labour-managed firms. Evidently, it is within closer reach of union power to push wages up than to pull the cost of capital down! The intersectoral and international mobility of financial capital is a source of immunity from organized influences, especially by labour. The threat of strike by the employees of a capitalist firm is apt to be more effective than the threat by members of a labour-managed firm to dispense with an equity issue! Monitoring labour markets is a much more natural target for a union than monitoring capital markets. And yet, the latter target would have to receive priority in the labour-managed economy. It is thus understandable that unions devote little energy to the promotion of labour management.

Second-best heuristics

It was noted in section 3.4 that efficient labour contracts should result in a degree of stability of workers' incomes comparable with the stability of returns to a diversified portfolio. And yet, for blue-collar workers subject to temporary or part-time layoffs, the contracts tend to stipulate instead some degree of stability for hourly wages (either nominal or real). It has been part of the strategies of organized labour to strive for income protection at a national level, through unemployment benefits, rather than at the firm level. I can see three reasons for this.

The first reason, just mentioned, is that labour organizations can often operate more effectively at that level, with greater strength and smaller transaction costs. The second reason is that not all firms are financed through equity floated on the stock market. For the smaller, more closely held firms, a national scheme of unemployment compensation is a form of risk-sharing between all members of the firm (owners and employees) and the rest of the economy. The third reason is that firms face risks of bankruptcy, so that protection of the workers is more effective when based on national schemes than when based at the firm level.

The combination of efficent economy-wide labour contracts and unemployment insurance strikes me, in the end, as a reasonable first step towards efficient risk-sharing, in the presence of uncertainty, incomplete markets and transaction costs. The last element, which is central to the explanation of market incompleteness, cannot be ignored when considering labour contracts. It would be fallacious to assume without justification that a difficulty standing in the way of market organization disappears altogether at the firm level.

Two complementary features were mentioned, which seem worth adding to that combination. In the smaller firms, not quoted on the stock exchange or otherwise included in the risk pool of capital markets, some participation of labour in the firm-specific risks makes sense; it should be accompanied with participation in managerial decisions. Limiting forms of participation include the bond-financed labour-managed firm, the partnership or the family enterprise. They flourish in the less capital-intensive sectors of our economies. In the larger firms, financed through the stock exchange and using contract labour, one would hope that the internal organization makes room for labour-managed or participatory decisions about working conditions.

A digression on working time

It is interesting to speculate, as a brief digression, about the extent to which the argument of collective pressure applies to working conditions as well as to income formation. The issue of working time is an intriguing case in point. Is the secular reduction in working time[4] a by-product of labour-market equilibrium, reflecting the equality of the reservation wage for hours and the marginal value product of labour according to equations (1.36) or (3.18); or is it an (explicit or implicit) component of union strategies to boost hourly wages? If the latter motivation were absent, and unions were eager to promote the welfare of their members (an acceptable hypothesis, in the small world where I live), then we should witness more union support for flexibility of individual working times.

5.3 A dynamic macroeconomic aspect

New entrants to the labour market

One important dimension of efficient risk-sharing between capital and labour is missing from my presentation so far. It concerns new entrants into the labour market. Bringing in that dimension explains why concern by labour organizations about the outcome of collective wage negotiations and the organization of economy-wide unemployment insurance is well placed. It provides a suggestive explanation of downward wage rigidity and unemployment, flowing from microeconomic considerations.

In the general equilibrium analysis of chapters 3 and 4, I focused on efficient risk-sharing through two-period labour contracts, assuming that the markets for such labour contracts cleared in the initial period. Spot markets for labour in the second period were not needed. In reality, however, a new generation of school leavers enters the market for labour contracts each year, whereas older workers go into retirement. In the streamlined models with only two explicit periods, the present and the future, there is a specific need to consider spot markets in the second period, if one wishes to include in the analysis these future entrants into the labour market. These spot markets stand in fact for markets for new labour contracts in the future.

That extension introduces an important feature, which does not seem to have received in the theoretical literature the attention which it deserves. Future entrants into the labour market are not present when multiperiod contracts are drawn, and the markets for such contracts clear, in an initial period. In other words, whereas long-term labour contracts are commonplace, we do not observe *forward labour contracts*, binding today a firm and a prospective worker on the terms of an employment relationship taking effect in the future. Consequently, future entrants into the labour market are left to bear fully the risks associated with labour-market conditions at their time of entry. They do not participate in the risk-sharing between capital and labour embodied in the extant long-term contracts.

To be more specific, think about an economy operating under conditions of technological uncertainty. Labour productivity tomorrow will depend upon the state of the environment, so that market-clearing wage levels will also depend upon that state. Labour contracts drawn today, and capital markets, organize risk-sharing among property owners and workers. If the technological developments are particularly adverse to labour (if they result in a very low marginal value product of labour at full employment), contract wages will be kept above the marginal product, in exchange for slightly lower wages today or in other states. But the future entrants, who are not covered by the terms of a forward contract, are not insured against that contingency. When contracting tomorrow, they will have to accept wages reflecting the marginal product of their labour in the state that obtains. Because market-clearing wages are apt to vary widely, and most prospective workers have no assets, that degree of income uncertainty is costly to bear, and should be alleviated through some mutually advantageous insurance supplied by property owners and workers under contract.

The absence of forward labour contracts means that such insurance is not organized at the microeconomic level of individual firms and individual workers. The difficulty of matching on a forward basis the future supply and demand of labour services at the firm level, and the even greater difficulty of organizing such matching on a contingent basis,[5] explain fully why each generation of new entrants has to look for jobs when the time comes. And there is no natural motivation for individual firms (whether capitalist or labour managed) to offer insurance against wage fluctuations to the anonymous set of prospective job seekers. By its very nature, that problem must be faced at the macroeconomic level. This is another interesting instance where microeconomic reasoning leads spontaneously to macroeconomic considerations – a situation for which I have an intimate liking.[6]

At the macroeconomic level, income insurance for new job seekers could be organized in either of two ways: namely general income maintenance programmes, or downward wage rigidity coupled with unemployment insurance. Both systems entail some costs. A general income maintenance programme, financed by taxes levied on property owners and employed workers, is costly on account of the distortive incidence of the taxes. Being a general programme, it has more beneficiaries than unemployment insurance; hence it typically calls for more tax revenue, creating more inefficiency on that score. On the other hand, downward wage rigidity results in wasteful underutilization of labour. The two sources of inefficiency must be compared, to decide which programme (or combination of programmes) is least inefficient. Also, the amount of insurance supplied to the newcomers will have to take these costs into account.

From the viewpoint of labour, a general income maintenance programme is less attractive, because its benefits are widely distributed. Also, it is not within the power of labour to organize such a programme. But labour organizations have indeed turned their efforts towards implementing downward wage rigidity coupled with unemployment insurance.[7] By its very nature, downward wage rigidity is a macroeconomic phenomenon; as a form of income insurance for newcomers, it is meaningless at the firm level.

Ex ante *efficient downwards wage rigidity*

What can be said about *efficient* provision of income insurance on behalf of newcomers through downward wage rigidity and unemployment benefits? A simple model, based on Drèze (1986), Gollier (1988) and joint work in progress by the two of us, is presented in appendix 5 to help investigate that novel question.

That model is meant to exhibit the simplest possible structure within which the issue can be discussed. It is accordingly an aggregate model, with a single good and a single aggregate production function whose shifts introduce 'technological uncertainty'. For simplicity, employment is the only argument of the production function. Investment and demand aspects are provisionally ignored, to concentrate on the insurance problem.

There are two generations of workers: an older generation, whose members are covered by labour contracts, the terms of which are state dependent, but set before observing the state; and a younger generation, whose members are hired after observing the state. For simplicitiy, I assume that all the older workers are employed under all states, and earn the state-dependent wages w_{0s} The wages $w_s \leqslant w_{0s}$ of the younger workers are also state dependent and set *ex ante*, but their employment level is determined *ex post* by equality between the wage and the marginal value product of labour (equal to the marginal physical product, upon normalizing to unity the price of the good in every state). Unemployed younger workers receive unemployment benefits $t_s \leqslant w_s$. (The conditions $t_s \leqslant w_s \leqslant w_{0s}$ are introduced for incentive compatibility.)

The wages w_{0s} and w_s are net of taxes and all workers have identical preferences, represented by the twice continuously differentiable utility function $u(w)$. These workers supply inelastically one unit of labour. There are L_0 older workers and L younger workers. The unemployment benefits are subtracted from the gross profits to define the property income

$$\pi_s = f_s(L_0 + L_s) - w_{0s}L_0 - w_sL_s - t_s(L - L_s) \qquad (5.1)$$

where $L_s \lessdot L$, the employment of younger workers, is such that

$$f_s'(L_0 + L_s) = w_s. \tag{5.2}$$

The preferences of property owners are represented by the utility function $V(\pi)$, best understood as reflecting portfolio choices, consistent for instance with the Capital Asset Pricing Model.

Using an undetermined parameter λ to represent the distributive choices between workers and property owners, the problem of defining *ex ante* Pareto-efficient wages and unemployment benefits becomes

$$\max_{w_{0s},\, w_s,\, t_s} \lambda E_s V[f_s(L_0 + L_s) - w_{0s}L_0 - w_sL_s - t_s(L - L_s)]$$
$$+ E_s[L_0u(w_{0s}) + L_su(w_s) + (L - L_s)u(t_s)] \tag{5.3}$$
$$\text{subject to } f_s'(L_0 + L_s) = w_s,\ L_s \leqslant L,\ w_{0s} \geqslant w_s \geqslant t_s.$$

The solution to this problem is best understood by looking successively at its implications for the older and for the younger generation.

For older workers under contract, efficient risk-sharing with property owners requires

$$u'(w_{0s}) = \lambda V'(\pi_s). \tag{5.4}$$

That is also the condition obtained in equation (3.16) as a characterization of an efficient contract at the firm level. (The simplification here comes from identical workers and anonymous shareholders.) Condition (5.4) prevails here, as long as $f_s'(L_0 + L) \leqslant w_{0s}$; that is, as long as it implies wages w_{0s} at least as high as the market-clearing wages for the younger generation. Otherwise (in very good states), the pressure of labour demand leads to wages higher than required by risk-sharing considerations, and determined by the conditions

$$f_s'(L_0 + L) = w_{0s} \qquad u'(w_{0s}) < \lambda V'(\pi_s). \tag{5.5}$$

In short, the wages of older workers correspond to the maximum of a risk-sharing wage and a market-clearing wage.

Turning to the younger generation, the solution assigns to them market-clearing wages, as long as these do not fall too much below the contractual wages. There is a maximal degree of intergenerational wage discrimination, endogenously determined, at which downward wage rigidity and unemployment set in. That solution has several interesting feature:

(i) Some degree of downward wage rigidity, leading to unemployment at positive wages (in bad states), is warranted on efficiency grounds.
(ii) The wages of newcomers are lower than those of workers under contract (wage discrimination by hiring date), unless there is full employment at wages higher than warranted by risk-sharing considerations for workers under contract; the degree of discrimination depends upon the wage elasticity of labour demand and upon the risk aversion of workers.
(iii) Unemployment benefits are equal to minimum wages, so that all unemployment is voluntary *ex post* from the individual viewpoint.

Some of these features reflect the specificity of the model. The more important point for my present purposes is the first, which validates the practice of downward wage rigidity as a 'second-best efficient' risk-sharing device. That conclusion seems quite robust, in models where future generations are not otherwise insured against fluctuations in market-clearing wages. It also validates the concern of labour unions about the strength of their bargaining position in collective wage settlements. The rest of the analysis does, however, confirm that prevailing wage determination schemes are not second-best efficient - a point to which I shall return later.

Looking at the first conclusion from another angle, one could say that economy-wide wage policies form an essential part of efficient risk-sharing between property owners and workers, when the interests of future generations of workers are taken into account. (When the third conclusion holds, wages and unemployment benefits are perfect substitutes as policy instruments.)

Wage discrimination by hiring date

It is interesting that I can write down explicitly, in this simple model, the conditions under which downward wage rigidity and unemployment set in. Assuming that contractual wages automatically satisfy condition (5.4), and market-clearing wages condition (5.2), one first observes from (ii) that wage discrimination by hiring date sets in as soon as market-clearing wages fall short of contractual wages. The reason for the discrimination is simply that wages of workers under contract can be kept above the market-clearing level without adverse implications for the employment of these workers (labour hoarding), whereas wages of new workers could not exceed the market-clearing level without generating unemployment. That unemployment would be wasteful, because the marginal product of labour is higher than the disutility of work (assumed non-existent in appendix 5, but easily introduced into the model, as verified in Gollier 1988). When market-clearing wages are close to the contractual wages reflecting efficient risk-sharing between workers and property owners, the inefficiency associated with unemployment would outweigh the gain in risk-sharing efficiency associated with higher wages for newcomers. These two considerations exactly outweigh each other, in the simple model under review, when

$$u'(w_s) = u'(w_{0s})(1 - \eta_{L_s w_s}) > u'(w_{0s}) \tag{5.6}$$

where $\eta_{L_s w_s}$ is the elasticity of new hirings with respect to the hiring wages.

The logic behind that condition can be explained as follows. Using (5.4), (5.2) and the definition of the elasticity, (5.6) is equivalent, at $L_s = L$, to

$$Lu'(w_s) = \lambda V'(\pi_s)\left[L - f_s'(L_0 + L)\ \frac{\mathrm{d}L_s}{\mathrm{d}w_s}\right]. \tag{5.7}$$

In (5.7), the left-hand side measures the utility gains to younger workers of receiving higher wages (higher by one unit). The right-hand side measures the utility loss to property owners of paying these higher wages to younger workers (alone). That utility loss comes from lower profits, due first to the extra unit of wages going to L workers, and next to the loss of output from lower employment; that loss of output is measured by the marginal product of labour times the change in labour demand. (Thus the elasticity comes into the formula to account for the waste associated with unemployment, not to account for any form of monopolistic behaviour.)

Condition (5.6) is stated in terms of the marginal utilities of workers under contract and of newcomers. Assuming identical preferences for both groups, and expanding marginal utilities in a Taylor series through quadratic terms, one can approximate (5.6) by the more operational condition

$$\dot{w}_s = w_{0s} \left[1 + \frac{\eta_{L_s w_s}}{R_R(w_{0s})} \right], \qquad \frac{w_{0s} - w_s}{w_{0s}} = \frac{|\eta_{L_s w_s}|}{R_R(w_{0s})}, \tag{5.8}$$

where $R_R(w_{0s})$ is the Arrow-Pratt measure of relative risk aversion for the workers, evaluated at the contractual wage.

It conforms to intuition that the loss associated with inefficient risk-sharing is a function of the degree of risk aversion of the workers. In the operational formula (5.8), the maximal relative wage discrimination by hiring date is directly proportional to the wage elasticity of labour demand by firms and inversely proportional to the risk aversion of workers. When that maximal discrimination separates contractual wages from market clearing wages, downward wage rigidity sets in to prevent further discrimination. The formula which applies from there on is a slight generalization of (5.6), namely

$$u'(w_s) = u'(w_{0s}) \left(1 - \frac{L_s}{L} \eta_{L_s w_s} \right) = u'(w_{0s}) \left(1 - w_s \frac{\mathrm{d}L_s}{\mathrm{d}w_s} \right). \tag{5.9}$$

It is interesting to speculate about the order of magnitude of the implied discrimination. To that effect, I note first that η_s, the wage elasticity of new hirings, is related to the wage elasticity of employment by the formula

$$\eta_s = \frac{w_s L_s'}{L_s} = \frac{w_s L_s'}{L_0 + L_s} \frac{L_0 + L_s}{L_s}.$$

That is, η_s is equal to the wage elasticity of employment times the ratio of total employment to new hirings. This is a fortunate feature, because it dispenses with the need to decide whether we should use a short- or a long-run elasticity number. As is well known, the orders or magnitude of the short-run and long-run elasticities of employment are quite different. According to Drèze and Modigliani (1981), for instance, the long-run elasticity could easily be 6 to 10 times as high as the short-run elasticity. But the ratio of total employment to new hirings is also very different in the two cases. According again to Belgian data, it is close to 6 on a yearly basis, whereas it should tend to 1 in the long run. Thus we may for practical purposes use the long-run wage elasticity of employment as an estimate of 'the' wage elasticity of new hirings. Unity is then a reasonable order of magnitude, even if the precision of our estimates leaves much to be desired. Hoping that L_s/L is reasonably close to unity as well, we would then conclude that the margin of wage discrimination is of the same order of magnitude as the reciprocal of the Arrow-Pratt relative risk-aversion measure for workers. Here again, we face an estimation problem. Casual appraisal of insurance deductibles suggests a margin of discrimination of the order of 20 per cent (a relative risk-aversion measure of the order of 5),[8] say plus or minus 5 per cent.

Could one translate conditions (5.4)–(5.8) into operational guidelines? Attempting to do so rigorously leads to complicated formulas of doubtful applicability. There is, however, one approximation conducive to major technical as well as logical simplification, which seems commensurate with the precision of available econometric estimates of the relevant parameters (namely the wage elasticity of employment and the relative risk-aversion measure). The approximation consists in treating the factor of proportionality between $u'(w_s)$ and $u'(w_{0s})$ in (5.9) as a constant – say $1/\mu$.[9] The solution is then entirely characterized by

$$u'(w_{0s}) = \lambda V'(\pi_s) = \mu u'(w_s) \tag{5.10}$$

whenever there is less than full employment. Equation (5.10) is of the same form as (3.21); it is simply a characterization of efficient risk-sharing between the three groups of agents: workers under contract, property owners and new entrants to the labour market. Implementing the solution is now a matter of achieving efficient risk-sharing through the labour contracts, linking the wage of new hires (and/or the unemployment benefits) to the contractual wages by means of formula (5.8), and hopefully letting demand pressure reduce the extent of discrimination at full employment. The resulting heuristic guidelines are basically the following.

Let the wages of workers under contract be determined by a simple economy-wide convention (like indexation in part on consumer prices and in part on nominal national income), giving content to the conditions (5.4) – or (3.16) – which characterize efficient risk-sharing between workers under contract and property owners. As long as market-clearing wages for all workers (those under contract and the new entrants) are equal to or higher than these contractual wages, the pressure of labour demand will result in full employment at these higher wages. When the market-clearing wages fall below the contractual level, wage discrimination between the workers under contract and the new workers sets in, with the new workers earning market-clearing wages, while the workers under contract continue to earn their (higher) contractual wages. That situation is allowed to prevail as long as the relative discrimination remains moderate – say not exceeding 20 per cent or so. When that level of discrimination is reached, downwards wage rigidity for the new workers sets in, and there results some (inefficient) unemployment, with unemployment benefits high enough to make the unemployment voluntary. The wages of the new workers, and the unemployment benefits, are then tied to the contractual wages, to which they remain proportional (though at the lower level corresponding to the maximal tolerated discrimination).

These guidelines are presented here as 'heuristic', first because they are derived within a very incomplete model, and second because they correspond to approximate and not to exact formulas. They should thus be regarded as *indicative* of the general nature of desirable policies, with no weight being attached to specific details.

Much simplicity of exposition is gained from assuming that prevailing long-term contracts are efficient, and from tailoring the wages of new workers to these contractual wages. The guidelines could thus be called 'operational'. This should not be allowed to conceal the need for characterizing efficient contracts as part of the policy. The simple indexation scheme proposed for illustration is indicative of desirable properties. Why it is not encountered in practice remains to be properly understood. That fact in itself is a ground for caution. Neither should one underestimate the practical difficulty of giving empirical content to the theoretical concept of market-clearing wages, a difficulty already mentioned in section 1.5. Several recent contributions to the theory of employment address that topic from different angles, like job search, efficiency wages, intertemporal labour–leisure substitution, insider–outsider differentials, and so on.[10] A common theme of these contributions is that the concept of market-clearing wages is by no means straightforward.

Complications

The analysis sketched here ignores several complications, among which the following three seem to be particularly significant.

First, the model of appendix 5 is a model of pure technological uncertainty, which ignores altogether demand and investment. Demand matters whenever observed unemployment has a Keynesian dimension, with output determined at least in part by aggregate demand, at a level where the marginal value product of labour exceeds the wages of marginal workers. It is then important to take into account the marginal propensities to spend wage income and property income respectively. And investment matters because the production possibilities (hence the marginal product of labour) are influenced by investments, as well as by the state of the environment. Once these considerations are introduced, the repercussions of the wage formation (and in particular of the downward wage rigidities) on employment become much more complex, and can only be spelled out in the framework of a complete macroeconomic model.[11] Such a task lies beyond the scope of this book. It is, of course, of paramount importance for policy choices.

Second, the present discussion is based entirely on a two-period model, that is on a simple dichotomy between the present and the future. In reality, history unfolds progressively: every day is part of the previous day's future, and is in turn endowed with its own future. The risk-sharing considerations introduced here must be embedded in a dynamic picture, with a view to characterize optimal paths.[12] The dynamics of intergenerational wage discrimination are an intriguing subject.

Third, the model of appendix 5 is an aggregate model, which ignores the diversity among firms, skills or sectors. In reality, one typically observes more diversity; some firms or sectors operate at full capacity and hire additional labour, while others experience excess capacities and hoard labour; and there are shortages of specialized skills in the midst of serious unemployment. That diversity is another source of complication, which restricts the immediate relevance of the aggregate guidelines drawn above.

Inegalitarian cooperatives

It is of some interest to relate, by way of a brief digression, conclusion (ii) (following (5.5)) regarding wage discrimination by hiring date, to a similar conclusion reached by Meade (1982) in his discussion of the promotion of employment in labour-managed cooperatives. Recognizing that labour-managed firms would not be inclined to take on new members, when the value added per member exceeds the reservation wage of outsiders, Meade advocates the principle of 'inegalitarian cooperatives', who take on new members at a lower share in value added than existing members, or possibly even at a market wage with employee status. This corresponds to the practice, witnessed in some Israeli kibbutzim and some Western cooperatives, of hiring salaried workers at wages inferior to the earnings of members. A macroeconomic justification for that practice is provided by the second conclusion just recalled. The fuller analysis here reveals under what conditions that practice is justified, and defines an upper bound on the degree of income discrimination warranted by efficiency considerations.

5.4 Overall conclusion

Putting together the conclusions collected in earlier sections of this chapter, I feel confident in formulating an overall conclusion.

In economies operating with uncertainty and incomplete insurance markets, it is natural to find capital hiring labour, because efficient labour contracts in capitalist firms are easier to draw and monitor than efficient equity contracts for labour-managed firms. That form of organization meets the preference of capitalists for vesting managerial authority with representatives of capital. It also meets the preference of labour organizations for acting on labour markets rather than on capital markets. It lends itself more naturally to economies of transaction costs through centralized negotiations over contracts (sectoral or economy-wide wage settlements). Finally, it lends itself naturally to the inclusion of future generations of workers in the risk-sharing arrangements between capital and labour, through downward wage rigidity and unemployment insurance.

It seems doubtful that labour contracts prevailing in capitalist economies correspond closely to efficient risk-sharing, because they fail to link labour incomes to aggregate wealth. (Constant real wages provide too much insurance, constant nominal wages potentially too little.) Improvements are possible, but may not be easy to implement. My main suggestion would be to index wages partly on consumer prices and partly on nominal national income. Smaller firms with closely held equity could be labour managed, if working conditions call for frequent and subtle adjustments, or could practise profit-sharing and participatory decision-making. The main challenge of the day, however, lies with improving the efficiency of collective wage bargaining.

Notes

1 The formal analogy between uncertainty and quality choices as instances of incomplete markets is brought out in Drèze and Hagen (1978).
2 That point is distinct from the point illustrated in section 4.2, to the effect that more developed capital markets may lead to better terms for labour contracts.
3 It is explained in Drèze and Modigliani (1972) that risk aversion is apt to increase with age.
4 The combination of shorter weekly hours, longer vacations and shorter careers has nearly halved lifetime working time over the past century; see for example Armstrong (1984) or Maddison (1982).
5 With how many firms would students need to contract on a contingent basis to be sure of having a job at the end of their studies? With how many students would a firm need to contract in order to cover contingent needs a few years hence?
6 See for example Drèze (1987b, p. 20) or Drèze (1985c, pp. 282–3).
7 Historically, unemployment insurance did not cover new entrants into the labour force until quite recently, and still does not cover them at all in many countries; see Emerson (1988).
8 See Drèze (1981). It would of course be improper to use here a relative risk-aversion measure based on portfolio choices of asset owners.
9 Those rigorous formulas which I could obtain suggest that the approximation introduces a bias in the elasticity of wages to national income (thus not in the wage level itself) which is definitely upward, but moderate (say of the order of 5 per cent).
10 See Lindbeck and Snower (1985) for a recent survey.
11 Of course, empirical estimates of the wage elasticity of employment hope to incorporate these repercussions. To that extent, they are implicitly incorporated here as well.
12 See Gollier (1988, chapter 2) for a multiperiod extension of the model in appendix 5.

Appendix 1

The following definitions were introduced in section 1.3.

Definition A.1

A *labour-management equilibrium for a market economy* (LME) is a tuple $(y^j, z^j) \in Y^j, j = 1, \ldots, J$; $(x^i, z^i) \in C^i$, $Z^i = [z_l^{ij}]$, an $L \times J$ matrix satisfying $\Sigma_j z_l^{ij} = z_l^i$, $l = 1, \ldots, L$, $i = 1, \ldots, I$; $p \in R_+^G$; $r \in R_+^J$; $A = [a_l^j]$, an $L \times J$ matrix with $a_l^j \geqslant 1 \; \forall j, l$, such that:

$$\sum_i x^i \leqslant \sum_i w^i + \sum_j y^j \tag{1.18}$$

$$\forall j, \quad \sum_i z^{ij} = z^j \tag{1.19}$$

$$\forall j, \quad V^j = \frac{py^j - r^j}{\sum_l a_l^j z_l^j} \geqslant \frac{p\bar{y}^j - r^j}{\sum_l a_l^j \bar{z}_l^j} \; \forall (\bar{y}^j, \bar{z}^j) \in Y^j \tag{1.14}$$

$$\forall i, \quad (x^i, z^i) \in B^i(p, z, A) \cap C^i \text{ and}$$

$$(x^i, z^i) \succsim_i (\bar{x}^i, \bar{z}^i) \; \forall (\bar{x}^i, \bar{z}^i) \in B^i(p, r, A) \cap C^i \tag{1.17}$$

where

$$B^i(p, r, A) = \{(x^i, z^i) \mid px^i \leqslant pw^i + \sum_l \sum_j z_l^{ij} a_l^j V^j + \sum_j \theta_{ij} r^j\}. \tag{1.16}$$

Writing $\omega \in \Omega$ for the $(J + 2I)$-tuple $((y^j, z^j), (x^i, z^i), Z^i)$, an LME is a tuple (ω, p, r, A) satisfying (1.14), (1.16)–(1.19).

Definition A.2

A *competitive equilibrium for a private ownership economy* (CE) is a triple $\omega \in \Omega$, $p \in R_+^G$, $s \in R_+^L$ satisfying (1.18) and (1.19) and such that

$$\forall j, \quad py^j - sz^j \geqslant p\bar{y}^j - s\bar{z}^j \quad \forall (\bar{y}^j, \bar{z}^j) \in Y^j \tag{1.21}$$

$$\forall i, \quad (x^i, z^i) \in B^i(p, z, A) \cap C^i \text{ and}$$

$$(x^i, z^i) \succsim_i (\bar{x}^i, \bar{z}^i) \, \forall (\bar{x}^i, \bar{z}^i) \in B^i(p,s) \cap C^i \tag{1.17$'$}$$

where

$$B^i(p,s) = \{(x^i, z^i) \,|\, px^i \leqslant pw^i + sz^i + \sum_j \theta_{ij}(py^j - sz^j)\}. \tag{1.22}$$

Standard results on competitive equilibria are found, for instance, in Debreu (1959). Consider the following assumptions (all i and j).

Assumption A.1

$C^i = C^i_G \times C^i_L$ is closed and convex, with $C^i_G \subset R^G_+$ and $C^i_L \subset R^L_+$; C^i_L is compact.

Assumption A.2

$\succsim_i$ is continuous and convex.

Assumption A.3

$x^i_g > \bar{x}^i_g \; \forall \, g$ implies $(x^i, z^i) \succ_i (\bar{x}^i, z^i) \; \forall \, (x^i, z^i), (\bar{x}^i, z^i) \in C^i$.

Assumption A.4

C^i_G owns x^i with $x^i_g < w^i_g \; \forall \, g$.

Assumption A.5

Y^j is closed and convex; $0 \in Y^j$.

Assumption A.6

$Y^j \cap (-Y^j) \subset \{0\}$; $(y^j, z^j) \in Y^j$ implies $(\bar{y}^j, z^j) \in Y^j \; \forall \, \bar{y}^j \leqslant y^j$.

Theorem A.1

Under assumptions A.1–A.6, there exists a CE.

Definition A.3

A Pareto optimum is an allocation $\omega \in \Omega$ such that there does not exist $\bar{\omega} \in \Omega$ with $(\bar{x}^i, \bar{z}^i) \succsim_i (x^i, z^i) \; \forall \, i$, $(\bar{x}^h, \bar{z}^h) \succ_h (x^h, z^h)$ for some h.

Theorem A.2

(i) Under assumption A.3, every CE is a Pareto optimum.
(ii) Under assumptions A.1–A.3 and A.5, if $\omega \in \Omega$ is a Pareto optimum, there exist $w^i \in R^G$, $i = 1, \ldots, I$, $p \in R^G_+$ and $s \in R^L_+$ such that (ω, p, s) is a CE relative to $w = (w^1, \ldots, w^I)$.

I now state and prove the two theorems on which section 1.3 rests.

Theorem A.3

Under assumption A.3, if (ω, p, r, A) defines an LME, there exists $s \in R^L_+$ such that (ω, p, s) is a CE.

Proof

The proof consists in defining a particular salary vector $s \in R^L_+$, then verifying that (1.14) and (1.17) in definition A.1 imply that (1.21) and (1.17)′ in definition A.2 are satisfied by (ω, p) and that s.

Let then s be defined by

$$s_l = \max_j V^j a^j_l \qquad l = 1, \ldots, L.$$

That is, the salary for labour of type l is taken equal to the highest earnings, $V^j a^j_l$, that can be obtained from any firm for that type of labour.

With s_l so defined, $l = 1, \ldots, L$, we first remark that $V^j a^j_l < s_l$ implies $z^j_l = \Sigma^I_{i=1} z^{ij}_l = 0$. Indeed, the monotonicity assumption A.3, and condition (1.17) in definition A.1, imply that no individual would supply labour of type l to a firm where his earnings would be less than the attainable alternative s_l, in equilibrium. Consequently,

$$\Sigma^L_{l=1} V^j a^j_l z^j_l = \Sigma^L_{l=1} s_l z^j_l \quad \text{for all } j = 1, \ldots, J$$

$$\Sigma^J_{j=1} V^j \, \Sigma^L_{l=1} a^j z^{ij}_l = \Sigma^L_{l=1} s_l z_l{}^i \quad \text{for all } i = 1, \ldots, I.$$

We now verify that, for each firm j, $py^j - sz^j \geqslant p\bar{y}^j - s\bar{z}^j$ for all $(\bar{y}^j, \bar{z}^j)$ in Y^j. Indeed, $V^j a_l^j \leqslant s_l$ for all l, or $V^j a^j \leqslant s$, implies

$$p\bar{y}^j - s\bar{z}^j \leqslant p\bar{y}^j - V^j a^j \bar{z}^j \equiv p\bar{y}^j - \frac{py^j - r^j}{a^j z^j} a^j \bar{z}^j$$

$$\equiv \left(\frac{p\bar{y}^j - r^j}{a^j \bar{z}^j} - \frac{py^j - r^j}{a^j z^j} \right) a^j \bar{z}^j + r^j \leqslant r^j$$

where the last inequality follows from condition (1.14) in definition A.1. Thus $p\bar{y}^j - s\bar{z}^j \leqslant r^j$ for all $(\bar{y}^j, \bar{z}^j)$ in Y^j (and this is true for all $j = 1, \ldots, J$).

On the other hand, $V^j a_l^j z_l^j = s_l z_l^j$ for all l implies

$$py^j - sz^j = py^j - V^j a^j z^j \equiv py^j - \frac{py^j - r^j}{a^j z^j} a^j z^j = r^j.$$

It then follows that $r^j = py^j - sz^j \geqslant p\bar{y}^j - s\bar{z}^j$ for all $(\bar{y}^j, \bar{z}^j)$ in Y^j, and condition (1.21) in definition A.2 is satisfied by (ω, p, s).

As for condition (1.17)′, it is also satisfied because the budget constraint $B^i(p, r, A)$ reduces to

$$px^i \leqslant pw^i + \sum_{l=1}^{L} s_l \sum_{j=1}^{J} z_l^{ij} + \sum_{j=1}^{J} \theta_{ij}(py^j - sz^j)$$

when $V^j a_l^j = s_l$ (or $z_l^{ij} = 0$) and $r^j = py^j - sz^j$. This is precisely the budget constraint $B^i(p, s)$, so that conditions (1.17) and (1.17)′ are identical and the proof is complete. □

The converse proposition is also true.

Theorem A.4

If (ω, p, s) defines a competitive equilibrium, then there exist (r, A) such that (ω, p, r, A) defines a labour-management equilibrium.

Proof

The proof is similar in spirit to that of theorem A.3, and will therefore be stated concisely.

For each firm j, define r^j, V^j and a^j as follows:

$$r^j = py^j - sz^j \ (= \text{profits at the CE})$$

$$V^j = \min_l s_l$$

$$a_l^j = s_l/V^j \qquad l = 1, \ldots, L, \qquad (a_l^j \geqslant 1 \text{ for all } l).$$

It follows from condition (1.21) of definition A.2 that $p\bar{y}^j - s\bar{z}^j \leqslant r^j$ for all $(\bar{y}^j, \bar{z}^j)$ in Y^j. Thus

$$p\bar{y}^j - r^j \leqslant s\bar{z}^j \equiv V^j a^j \bar{z}^j$$

$$\frac{p\bar{y}^j - r^j}{a^j\bar{z}^j} \leqslant V^j \equiv \frac{s_l}{a_l^j} \equiv \frac{\sum_{l=1}^{L} s_l z_l^j}{\sum_{l=1}^{L} a_l^j z_l^j} \equiv \frac{py^j - r^j}{a^j z^j}$$

so that condition (1.14) of definition A.1 is satisfied.

Conditions (1.17) and (1.17)′ are again shown to be equivalent because the budget constraints $B^i(p,s)$ and $B^i(p,r,A)$ are identical, under the chosen definitions of r^j and $V^j a_l^j$. □

As immediate corollaries of theorems A.3 and A.4, we have the following.

Corollary A.1

Under assumption A.3, the sets of allocations that can be sustained as competitive equilibria and as labour-management equilibria are identical.

Corollary A.2

(i) Under assumption A.3, every LME is a Pareto optimum.
(ii) Under assumptions A.1–A.3 and A.5, if $\omega \in \Omega$ is a Pareto optimum, there exist $w^i \in R^G$, $i = 1, \ldots, I$, p, r and A such that (ω, p, r, A) is an LME relative to $w = (w^1, \ldots, w^I)$.

Corollary A.3

Under assumptions A.1–A.6, there exists an LME.

Remark

For all j such that $Y^j \supseteq (Y^j + Y^j)$, $py^j - sz^j = 0$ at a CE and $r^j = 0$ at an LME.

Finally, as an aid towards interpretation of theorem A.3, consider the special case where the production sets Y^j are defined by means of differentiable production functions. That is, consider the following.

Assumption A.7

For each j, there exists a differentiable function $f^j(y^j,z^j)$, such that $f^j(y^j,z^j) \leqslant 0$ for all (y^j,z^j) in Y^j, and $f^j(y^j,z^j) = 0$ on the efficient boundary of Y^j.

Theorem A.5

Under assumption A.7, if $(\omega,p,r,A,\{Z^i\})$ defines a labour-management equilibrium, then $z_l^j > 0$ implies that $V^j a_l^j$ is equal to the marginal value product of labour of type l in firm j, $l = 1, \ldots, L$, $j = 1, \ldots, J$.

Proof

A necessary condition for $V^j = py^j - r^j/a^j z^j$ to be maximal is that, when $z_l^j > 0$,

$$0 = \frac{\partial V^j}{\partial z_l^j} = \left[\frac{\partial (py^j)}{\partial z_l^j} \; a^j z^j - (py^j - r^j) a_l^j \right] \Bigg/ (a^j z^j)^2$$

or

$$\frac{\partial (py^j)}{\partial z_l^j} = \frac{py^j - r^j}{a^j z^j} \, a_l^j = V^j a_l^j .$$

Under our differentiability assumption, $\partial(py^j)/\partial z_l^j$ is the marginal value product of labour of type l in firm j. □

Appendix 2

In this appendix I prove the theorems given in chapter 2.[1] The model used in section 2.2 is as follows. There are $S+1$ commodities, indexed $s = 0, 1, \ldots, S$. There are J firms indexed $j = 1, \ldots, J$, with production sets $Y^j \subset R \times R^S_+$.

Assumption A.8

For each j, Y^j is closed convex; $0 \in Y^J$; the set $\{y^j \in Y^j | y^j_0 = c\}$ is compact, for all c in R; there exists $\bar{y}^j_0 < +\infty$, such that $y^j_0 \leqslant \bar{y}^j_0$ for all $y^j \in Y^j$.

A set of production plans for all firms is a vector

$$y = (y^1, \ldots, y^j, \ldots, y^J) \in \prod_{j=1}^{J} Y^j = \text{def } Y.$$

There are I consumers indexed $i = 1, \ldots, I$, with consumption sets $C^i \subset R^{S+1}_+$ and initial endowments w^i in R^{S+1}_+.

Assumption A.9

For each i, $C^i = R^{S+1}_+$ and $w^i \in \text{int } R^{S+1}_+$; the preference ordering $\succsim_i$ on C^i is continuous and convex; $x^i \geqslant \tilde{x}^i$ implies $x^i \succsim_i \tilde{x}^i$; $x^i \geqslant \tilde{x}^i$, with either $x^i_0 > \tilde{x}^i_0$ or $x^i_s > \tilde{x}^i_s$ for all $s = 1, \ldots, S$, implies $x^i \succ_i \tilde{x}^i$.

Shares of stock in the J firms are traded on a stock exchange against commodity 0. A price vector is a p in $\Delta = \{p \in R_+^{J+1} | \Sigma_{j=0}^J p_j = 1\}$. The initial holdings of shares are defined by a non-negative $I \times J$ matrix $\bar{\Theta}$ with $\Sigma_{i=1}^I \bar{\theta}_{ij} = 1, j = 1, \ldots, J$. Final holdings are denoted by Θ, with $1 \geqslant \theta_{ij} \geqslant 0 \ \forall \ i,j$, and $\Sigma_i \theta_{ij} = 1 \ \forall \ j$ in equilibrium. The set of non-negative $I \times J$ matrices with unit column sums is denoted $\mathcal{M}$. I write θ_i for row i of Θ, θ^j for column j of Θ.

Final holding of a share θ_{ij} of firm j entails an immediate expenditure equal to $\theta_{ij}(p_j - p_0 y_0^j)$ and gives right to a vector of 'dividends' $\theta_{ij} y_s^j$, $s = 1, \ldots, S$.

The final consumption of consumer i is a vector $x^i \in R_+^{S+1}$ satisfying

$$p_0 x_0^i + \sum_j \theta_{ij}(p_j - p_0 y_0^j) \leqslant p_0 w_0^i + \sum_j \bar{\theta}_{ij} p_j \tag{A.1}$$

$$x_s^i \leqslant w_s^i + \sum_j \theta_{ij} y_s^j \qquad s = 1, \ldots, S. \tag{A.2}$$

In view of the monotonicity of preferences, I shall proceed with θ_i as the only decision variable of consumer i. I shall write $x^i(\theta_i, p, y)$, or $x^i(\Theta, p, y)$, for the vector x^i defined by equality in (A.2) and either equality in (A.1) with $p_0 > 0$, or $x_0^i = +\infty$ with $p_0 = 0$. The constraint imposed on θ_i by the non-negativity of x_0^i is

$$\sum_j \theta_{ij}(p_j - p_0 y_0^j) \leqslant p_0 w_0^i + \sum_j \bar{\theta}_{ij} p_j. \tag{A.3}$$

I shall first prove theorem 2.2; as remarked in the text, theorem 2.1 then follows as an immediate corollary.[2] Accordingly, I define the *control groups* and introduce their properties.

For each firm j, there exists a correspondence $\mathcal{I}^j(\Theta): \mathcal{M} \rightarrow \{1, \ldots, i, \ldots, I\}$, with $\mathcal{I}^j(\Theta) \neq \phi$ for all $\Theta \in \mathcal{M}$ and $\theta_{ij} > 0$ for all $i \in \mathcal{I}^j(\Theta)$. That correspondence satisfies a continuity assumption, which can be given three equivalent, alternative formulations (form CC is in chapter 2).

Assumption CC′

For each $j = 1, \ldots, J$, the correspondence $\mathcal{I}^j(\Theta)$ is upper hemi-continuous for the discrete topology.

Assumption CC″

For each $j = 1, \ldots, J$, for each $\Theta \in \mathcal{M}$, these exists an open neighbourhood $B^j(\Theta)$, such that $\mathcal{I}^j(\Theta') \subseteq \mathcal{I}^j(\Theta)$ for all $\Theta' \in B^j(\Theta)$.

Assumption CC

For each $j = 1, \ldots, J$, for each $i = 1, \ldots, I$, the set $\{\Theta \in \mathcal{M} \mid i \in \mathcal{I}^j(\Theta)\}$ is closed.

Examples of correspondences verifying assumption CC′ include the following:

(i) $\mathcal{I}^j(\Theta)$ consists of all i such that $\theta_{ij} \geqslant \alpha$, for some $\alpha \in (0, 1/I]$.
(ii) $\mathcal{I}^j(\Theta)$ consists of the K leading shareholders, with tie-breaking by the union rule; that is, $\mathcal{I}^j(\Theta)$ is the union of all sets $\mathcal{I}_K$ with exactly K elements and such that $\theta_{ij} \geqslant \theta_{hj}$ for all $i \in \mathcal{I}_K$, $h \notin \mathcal{I}_K$.
(iii) $\mathcal{I}^j(\Theta)$ is the smallest set for which $\Sigma_i(\theta_{ij}: i \in \mathcal{I}^j(\Theta)) \geqslant \beta > 0$ with tie-breaking by the union rule; that is, if K is the smallest integer for which there exists a set $\mathcal{I}_K$ with exactly K elements such that $\Sigma_i(\theta_{ij}: i \in \mathcal{I}_K) \geqslant \beta$, then $\mathcal{I}^j(\Theta)$ is the union of all such sets.

See the appendix in Drèze (1985b) for graphical illustrations.

According to definition 2.2, a preference relation for firm j can then be defined as follows (conditionally on Θ):

$$\begin{aligned} &\hat{y}^j >_j y^j \text{ if there exists } \hat{\mathcal{I}}^j \subseteq \{1, \ldots, I\} \\ &\text{with } \mathcal{I}^j(\Theta) \subseteq \hat{\mathcal{I}}^j, \quad \Sigma_i(\theta_{ij}: i \in \hat{\mathcal{I}}^j) > 1/2, \\ &\quad x^i + \theta_{ij}(\hat{y}^j - y^j) >_i x^i \text{ for all } i \in \hat{\mathcal{I}}^j. \end{aligned} \tag{A.4}$$

For the purposes of the existence proof below, the domains of definition of the correspondences $\mathcal{I}^j(\Theta)$, and of the preference relations (A.4), must be extended from $\Theta \in \mathcal{M}$ to $\Theta \in \mathcal{M}^* := \{\Theta \mid 1 \geqslant \theta_{ij} \geqslant 0, i = 1, \ldots, I, j = 1, \ldots, J\}$; and the extension must preserve the upper hemicontinuity of the correspondences $\mathcal{I}^j(\Theta)$. A satisfactory extension is introduced in the proof of the theorem. One unavoidable implication is, however, that $\Sigma_i \theta_{ij} = 0$ implies $\{\hat{y}^j \mid \hat{y}^j >_j y^j\} = \phi$ for all y^j. As a consequence, a trivial equilibrium with for all j, $y^j = 0$ and $\Sigma_i \theta_{ij} = 0$, always exists.

In order to avoid that degeneracy, the proof of theorem 2.2 proceeds in two steps. I first impose that shareholders do not divest themselves entirely of their initial holdings, by adding the conditions $\theta_i \geq \epsilon\bar{\theta}_i$, where $\epsilon > 0$ is small enough that the set of feasible portfolios is non-empty, $i = 1, \ldots, I$. That set is defined by

$$T_i^\epsilon(p,y) = \{\theta_i | \forall j, 1 \geqslant \theta_{ij} \geqslant \epsilon\bar{\theta}_{ij};$$
$$\Sigma_j \theta_{ij}(p_j - p_0 y_0^j) \leqslant p_0 w_j^i + \Sigma_j \bar{\theta}_{ij} p_j\}. \qquad (A.5)$$

(When $\epsilon = 0$, $T_i(p,y)$ is the feasible set of the original economy.)

Existence of an equilibrium is obtained for the ϵ-economy so defined. In a second step, I consider a sequence ϵ^ν, $\nu = 1, 2, \ldots$, with $\lim_{\nu\to\infty} \epsilon^\nu = 0$; and a sequence of equilibria for the respective ϵ^ν-economies. The limit of such a sequence of equilibria is an equilibrium for the original economy.[3]

An *equilibrium of production and exchange for the control principle* (or EPE for definition 2.2) is a triple (y,p,Θ) satisfying:

(i) For each i, $\theta_i \in T_i(p,y)$ and there does not exist $\hat{\theta}_i \in T_i(p,y)$ with $x^i(\hat{\theta}_i,p,y) \succ_i x^i(\theta_i,p,y)$.
(ii) $p \in \Delta$ and $\Theta \in \mathcal{M}$.
(iii) For each j, $y^j \in Y^j$ and there do not exist $\hat{y}^j \in Y^j, \hat{\mathcal{F}}^j \subseteq \{1, \ldots, I\}$ with $\mathcal{F}^j(\Theta) \subseteq \hat{\mathcal{F}}^j$, $\Sigma_i(\theta_{ij}: i \in \hat{\mathcal{F}}^j) > 1/2$ and $x^i + \theta_{ij}(\hat{y}^j - y^j) \succ_i x^i$ $\forall\, i \in \hat{\mathcal{F}}^j$.

Theorem 2.2

Under assumptions A.8, A.9 and CC′, there exists an EPE for definition 2.2.

Proof

The proof is an application of the existence theorem for 'Equilibrium in abstract economies without ordered preferences' (Shafer and Sonneschein 1975), whose notation will be followed.

I first prove existence of an EPE in an ϵ-economy, $\epsilon > 0$. The abstract ϵ-economy consists of $N = I + J + 1$ agents. The first I agents, denoted i $(= 1, \ldots, I)$, correspond to the consumers, with choice sets $X_i = \{\theta_i | \forall_j, 1 \geqslant \theta_{ij} \geqslant 0\}$ of elements $(x_i =)\ \theta_i$, constraint correspondences $\mathcal{A}_i(x) = T_i^\epsilon(p,y)$ and preference correspondences $P_i(x) = \{\hat{\theta}_i \in X_i | x^i(\hat{\theta}_i,p,y) \succ_i x^i(\theta_i,p,y)\}$.

The next J agents, denoted $j = I + 1, \ldots, I + J$, correspond to the firms (reindexed $I + 1, \ldots, I + J$) with choice sets $X_j = Y^j$ of elements $(x_j =)\ y^j$, constraint correspondences $\mathcal{A}_j(x) = Y^j$ and preference correspondences defined as follows:

$$\text{if } \sum_i \theta_{ij} = 1:$$
$$P_j(x) = \{\hat{y} \in Y^j \mid \exists \hat{\mathscr{I}}^j: \mathscr{I}^j(\Theta) \subseteq \hat{\mathscr{I}}^j, \sum_i(\theta_{ij}: i \in \hat{\mathscr{I}}^j) > 1/2,$$
$$x^i + \theta_{ij}(\hat{y}^j - y^j) \succ_i x^i \ \forall\, i \in \hat{\mathscr{I}}^j\} \tag{A.6}$$
$$\text{if } 1 \neq \sum_i \theta_{ij} \geqslant \epsilon: \text{let } \tilde{\theta}_{ij} = \theta_{ij}/\sum_h \theta_{hj},\ \tilde{y}^j = \sum_i \theta_{ij} y^j,\ \tilde{\Theta} = [\tilde{\theta}_{ij}];$$
$$P_j(x) = \{\hat{y}^j \in Y^j \mid \exists \hat{\mathscr{I}}^j: \mathscr{I}^j(\tilde{\Theta}) \subseteq \hat{\mathscr{I}}^j, \sum_i(\tilde{\theta}_{ij}: i \in \hat{\mathscr{I}}^j) > 1/2,$$
$$x^i + \tilde{\theta}_{ij}(\hat{y}^j - \tilde{y}^j) \succ_i x^i \ \forall\, i \in \hat{\mathscr{I}}^j\}. \tag{A.7}$$

Although (A.6) is a special case of (A.7), it is written down separately to facilitate understanding. Note that the last condition in (A.7) is equivalent to

$$x^i + \theta_{ij}\left[\frac{1}{\Sigma_h \theta_{hj}}\hat{y}^j - y^j\right] \succ_i x^i \ \forall\, i \in \hat{\mathscr{I}}^j.$$

Agent $N = I + J + 1$ is the 'market agent' with choice set $X_N = \Delta$ of elements $(x_N =)\ p$, constraint correspondence $\mathscr{A}_N(x) \equiv \Delta$ and a preference correspondence defined by

$$P_N(x) = \{\hat{p} \in \Delta \mid (\hat{p}_0 - p_0)(\sum_i x_0^i - \sum_i \sum_j \theta_{ij} y_0^j - \sum_i w_0^i)$$
$$+ \sum_j (\hat{p}_j - p_j)(\sum_i \theta_{ij} - 1) > 0\}. \tag{A.8}$$

The abstract economy so defined is easily fitted into the Shafer-Sonnenschein framework. First, for each agent $h = 1, \ldots, N$, X_h is a non-empty closed and convex subset of R^l, where $l = IJ + (S+1)J + J + 1$, and R^l is the space of (Θ, y, p). Standard techniques for bounding X_h are applicable since $\Sigma_i w_0^i$ is finite and the cut of each Y^j at $y_0^j > -\infty$ is bounded.[4] Let then

$$X = \underset{h=1,\ldots,N}{\times} X_h$$

a compact set. It is understood that ϵ is small enough that

$$T_i^\epsilon(p,y) \neq \phi \quad \text{for all } p \in \Delta,\ \ y \in \underset{j=I+1,\ldots,I+J}{\times} Y_j .$$

The constraint correspondences of the consumers are continuous at all p such that $p_0 > 0$. One can thus use the standard technique of quasi-equilibria in Greenberg (1977), with $\psi_i(x) = p_0$. It is shown later that $p_0 > 0$ at a quasi-equilibrium, so that every quasi-equilibrium is an equilibrium. The constraint correspondences of the firms and of N are constant. That $\mathscr{A}_i(x)$ is non-empty and convex for all i and x is readily verified.

There remains to verify that the preference correspondences have an open graph, and satisfy the condition that x_i does not belong to the convex hull of $P_i(x)$, denoted $H(P_i(x))$, $i = 1, \ldots, N$. For $i = 1, \ldots, I$, the continuity and convexity of $\succsim_i$, plus the linearity of (A.1) and (A.2) in θ_i, imply that P_i has an open graph and is convex valued.

Consider next $j = I+1, \ldots, I+J$. Writing comp A for the complement of a set A, an alternative statement of (A.7) is:

$$\begin{aligned} P_j(x) &= \{\hat{y}^j \in Y^j \mid x^i + \tilde{\theta}_{ij}(\hat{y}^j - \tilde{y}^j) \succ_i x^i \ \forall\, i \in \mathscr{I}^j(\tilde{\theta}^j)\} \\ &\quad \cap \text{comp}\,\{\mathring{y}^j \in Y^j \mid \exists \mathring{\mathscr{I}}^j : \Sigma_i(\tilde{\theta}_{ij} : i \in \mathring{\mathscr{I}}^j) \geqslant 1/2, \\ &\qquad x^i \succsim_i x^i + \tilde{\theta}_{ij}(\mathring{y}^j - \tilde{y}^j) \ \forall\, i \in \mathring{\mathscr{I}}^j\} \qquad \text{(A.7)}' \\ &= \text{def } P_j^*(x) \cap \text{comp } P_j^0(x). \end{aligned}$$

The set $P_j^*(x)$ is an intersection, overall i $\in \mathscr{I}^j(\tilde{\theta}^j)$, of relative open convex sets; hence it is an open convex set.[5] $P_j^o(x)$ is the union, over all sets $\mathring{\mathscr{I}}^j$ with the required properties, of the intersections, over all i in $\mathring{\mathscr{I}}^j$, of closed sets; hence $P_j^o(x)$ is closed, as a finite union of closed sets; and $P_j(x)$ is open, as the relative complement in the open set $P_j^*(x)$ of the closed set $P_j^o(x)$. Although $P_j(x)$ is in general not convex, it is contained in the convex set $P^*(x)$ and y^j does not belong to the convex hull of $P_j^*(x)$, hence it does not belong either to that of $P_j(x) \subseteq P_j^*(x)$.

To say that P_j has an open graph is to say that, for all $(x, \hat{y}^j)$ in $X \times X_j$ with $\hat{y}^j \in P_j(x)$, there exists an open neighbourhood $B = B(x, \hat{y}^j)$ in $X \times X_j$ such that $(x', \hat{y}'^j) \in B$ implies $\hat{y}'^j \in P_j(x')$. Now, for each j, $\tilde{\theta}^j$ is a continuous function of θ^j on $R_+^I \setminus \{0\}$, and $\tilde{y}^j$ is a continuous function of θ^j and y^j on $R_+^I \times R^{(S+1)}$; clearly open neighbourhoods of (Θ, y) in $(R_+^{IJ} \setminus \{0\}) \times Y$ are mapped into open neighbourhoods of $(\tilde{\Theta}, \tilde{y})$ in $\mathscr{M} \times R^{(S+1)J}$. If x' is such that $\Theta' = \Theta$ (hence $\tilde{\Theta}' = \tilde{\Theta}$), and $x^i + \tilde{\theta}_{ij}(\hat{y}'^j - \tilde{y}^j) \succ_i x^i \ \forall\, i \in \hat{\mathscr{I}}^j$, then by continuity of preferences, for B small enough, for all $(x', \hat{y}'^j) \in B$, $x'^i + \tilde{\theta}_{ij}(\hat{y}'^j - \tilde{y}'^j) \succ_i x'^i \ \forall\, i \in \hat{\mathscr{I}}^j$. If $(x', \hat{y}'^j) \in B$ with $\Theta' \neq \Theta$, then for B small enough, assumption CC″ entails $\mathscr{I}^j(\tilde{\Theta}') \subseteq \mathscr{I}^j(\tilde{\Theta})$, so that $\mathscr{I}^j(\tilde{\Theta}') \subseteq \hat{\mathscr{I}}^j$; also $\Sigma_i(\tilde{\theta}'_{ij} : i \in \hat{\mathscr{I}}^j) > 1/2$, so that $x'^i + \tilde{\theta}_{ij}(\hat{y}'^j - \tilde{y}'^j) \succ_i x'^i \ \forall\, i \in \hat{\mathscr{I}}^j$ implies $\hat{y}'^j \in P_j(x')$. Thus, for all x such that $\Sigma_i\, \theta_{ij} > 0$, P_j has the desired properties; and $\Sigma_i\, \theta_{ij} \geqslant \epsilon > 0$ in the ϵ-economy.

Finally, $P_N(x)$ is clearly an open convex set, and P_N has an open graph.

Thus, all the conditions for the Shafer-Sonnenschein-Greenberg theorem are satisfied and there exists a triple (Θ, y, p) satisfying for each $i = 1, \ldots, N$, $x_i \in \mathscr{A}_i(x)$, and $P_i(x) \cap \mathscr{A}_i(x) = \phi$ provided $p_0 > 0$. There remains to verify that this triple defines an EPE for definition 2.2. I now show that $(\tilde{\Theta}, \tilde{y}, p)$ is such an EPE, where, for all i and j,

$$\tilde{\theta}_{ij} = \frac{\theta_{ij}}{\sum_h \theta_{hj}} \qquad \tilde{y}^j = \sum_h \theta_{hj} y^j. \tag{A.9}$$

Note that $\tilde{\theta}_{ij}\tilde{y}^j = \theta_{ij}y^j$ for all i and j, under (A.9); and $\tilde{y}^j \in Y^j$ whenever $\Sigma_i \theta_{ij} \leqslant 1$.

I first use (A.8) to verify that $p_0 > 0$, $\Sigma_{j=1}^J p_j < 1$. Indeed, from assumption A.9 (strict monotonicity of $\succsim_i$ with respect to x_0^i), $p_0 = 0$ would imply unlimited demands for x_0. Let b denote the upper bound placed on every variable in constructing the bounded economy, an arbitrarily large positive quantity. Then $x_0^i = b$ for all $i = 1, \ldots, I$. Because $1 \geqslant \theta_{ij} \geqslant 0$ for all i and j, and $y_0^j \leqslant \bar{y}_0^j$ for all j, $\Sigma_{ij}\theta_{ij}y_0^j \leqslant I\Sigma_j\bar{y}_0^j$. Thus $\Sigma_i x_0^i - \Sigma_{ij}\theta_{ij}y_0^j - \Sigma_i w_0^i \geqslant Ib - I\Sigma_j\bar{y}_0^j - \Sigma_i w_0^i$ will be an arbitrarily large positive quantity, when $p_0 = 0$. On the other hand, for all j, $\Sigma_i \theta_{ij} - 1 \leqslant I - 1$. Thus $P_N(x)$ would contain a $\hat{p}$ with $\hat{p}_0 = 1$, a contradiction. Thus, $p_0 > 0$ and $p_j < 1$ for all $j = 1, \ldots, J$. Also, $\psi_i(x) > 0$ for all $i = 1, \ldots, I$, implying $P_i(x) \cap \mathscr{A}_i(x) = \phi$.

With $p_0 > 0$, condition (A.1) holds as equality for each i, implying

$$p_0(\Sigma_i x_0^i - \Sigma_i\Sigma_j\theta_{ij}y_0^j - \Sigma_i w_0^i) + \Sigma_j p_j(\Sigma_i\theta_{ij} - 1) = 0, \tag{A.10}$$

where use has been made of $\Sigma_i \bar{\theta}_{ij} = 1 \; \forall j$. Substituting into (A.8), we have

$$P_N(x) = \{\hat{p} \in \Delta \,|\, \hat{p}_0(\Sigma_i x_0^i - \Sigma_i \Sigma_j \theta_{ij}y_0^j - \Sigma_i w_0^i) + \Sigma_j \hat{p}_j(\Sigma_i \theta_{ij} - 1) > 0\}. \tag{A.8$'$}$$

Therefore, $P_N(x) \cap \Delta = \phi$ implies that

$$\Sigma_i x_0^i - \Sigma_i \Sigma_j \theta_{ij}y_0^j - \Sigma_i w_0^i = \Sigma_i x_0^i - \Sigma_j \tilde{y}_0^j - \Sigma_i w_0^i \leqslant 0 \tag{A.11}$$

$$\Sigma_i \theta_{ij} \leqslant 1 \qquad j = 1, \ldots, J. \tag{A.12}$$

Using these two inequalities in (A.10), it follows that, for all j, either $p_j = 0$ or $\Sigma_i \theta_{ij} = 1$.

Also, (A.12) implies that $\tilde{y}^j \in Y^j$, $j = 1, \ldots, J$. This, together with (A.11), guarantees that $(\tilde{\Theta}, \tilde{y})$ defines a feasible allocation at which condition (ii) in the definition of an EPE for definition 2.2 is satisfied.

That condition (i) in that definition also holds follows directly from the definitions of $\mathscr{A}_i(x)$ and $P_i(x)$; the equilibrium property that $\mathscr{A}_i(x) \cap P_i(x) = \phi$, $i = 1, \ldots, I$, is precisely condition (i).

As for condition (iii) in the definition, it is clearly satisfied when $\Sigma_i \theta_{ij} = 1$, since it is then equivalent to $\mathscr{A}_j(x) \cap P_j(x) = \phi$, under definition (A.6). When $0 < \Sigma_i \theta_{ij} < 1$, then $\tilde{y}^j = \Sigma_i \theta_{ij} y^j \in Y^j$ satisfies condition (iii), since by (A.7) Y^j does not own $\hat{y}^j$ with $x^i + \tilde{\theta}_{ij}(\hat{y}^j - \tilde{y}^j) >_i x^i \; \forall \; i \in \hat{\mathscr{F}}^j$. Therefore, $(\tilde{\Theta}, \tilde{y}, p)$ as defined is an EPE for definition 2.2 in the ϵ-economy.

Let $(\tilde{\Theta}^\nu, \tilde{y}^\nu, p^\nu)$, $\nu = 1, 2, \ldots$, define a sequence of such equilibria in the ϵ^ν-economies, with $\lim_{\nu \to \infty} \epsilon^\nu = 0$. Because $(\tilde{\Theta}^\nu, \tilde{y}^\nu, p^\nu)$ belong $\forall \; \nu$ to the same compact set (corresponding to $\epsilon = 0$), there exist converging subsequences. Let $(\bar{\Theta}, \bar{y}, \bar{p})$ be the limit of such a subsequence. Then $(\bar{\Theta}, \bar{y}, \bar{p})$ is an EPE for definition 2.2 in the original economy.

In order to establish that property, it is necessary to show that $\bar{p} > 0$, so that $\forall \; i$, $T_i(p, y)$ is continuous at $\bar{p}, \bar{y}$ (because $w_0^i > 0$) and $\bar{\theta}_i$ satisfies there condition (i) of the definition of an EPE (because $\succsim_i$ is continuous). If it were the case that $\bar{p}_0 = 0$, then, because $p^\nu \in \Delta \; \forall \nu$ and because the number J of firms is finite, there would exist a firm j for which $\bar{p}_j > 0$ with $p_j^\nu > 0 \; \forall \; \nu$ along a subsequence. For some i with $\bar{\theta}_{ij} > 0$, it would be the case that $T_i(p, y)$ is continuous at $\bar{p}, \bar{y}$. The sequence of optimal portfolios θ_i^ν implies a sequence of consumption vectors $x^{i\nu}$ such that, for each ν, $x^{i\nu}$ is optimal for $\succsim_i$ subject to (A.1) and (A.2) given (p^ν, y^ν), and $\bar{x}^i$ is similarly optimal given $(\bar{p}, \bar{y})$. Hence, $\bar{x}_0^i = b$ and $x_0^{i\nu}$ is arbitrarily close to b for large ν, implying $p_0^\nu = 1$ by the argument already used in the first part of the proof to establish $p_0 > 0$. But this would imply $\bar{p}_0 = 1$, contradicting $\bar{p}_0 = 0$. Hence $\bar{p}_0 > 0$ and condition (i) in the definition of an EPE is verified at $(\bar{\Theta}, \bar{y}, \bar{p})$.

That condition (ii) also holds is immediate. As for condition (iii), it follows from closedness of Y and from the fact that, for each j, P_j has an open graph as shown above. If condition (iii) were violated at $(\bar{\Theta}, \bar{y}, \bar{p})$ then it would also be violated at $(\Theta^\nu, y^\nu, p^\nu)$ close enough to $(\bar{\Theta}, \bar{y}, \bar{p})$. This completes the proof of theorem 2.2. □

Notes

1 I am indebted to Bernard Cornet for suggesting several improvements in the presentation of appendix 2. The responsibility for remaining shortcomings is entirely mine.

2 Of course, theorem 2.1 does not require the special assumption CC′ to follow – but minor modifications in the proof are then needed, which did not seem worth spelling out.

3 In the 1983 manuscript of the Jahnsson Lectures, I introduced an *assumption* akin to $\theta_i \geqslant \epsilon\bar{\theta}_i$ (though weaker). The idea of the sequence was suggested by John Geanakoplos and is used in Geanakoplos et al. (1987).

4 See Debreu (1959, pp. 45–6).

5 From now on, 'open' is to be understood as 'relative open'.

Appendix 3

In this appendix I extend the reasoning of appendix 2 to prove the theorems given in chapter 3. Turning to the model used in that chapter, there are now $S + 1$ commodities and $S + 1$ labour services, indexed $s = 0, 1, \ldots, S$ in both cases. The J firms, indexed j, have production sets $Y^j \subset R^{2(S+1)}$, with elements (y^j, z^j), where $y^j \in R \times R^S_+$ and $z^j \in R^{S+1}_+$.

Assumption A.10

For each j, Y^j is closed convex, $0 \in Y^j$; the set $\{(y^j, z^j) \in Y^j \mid y^j_0 = c, z^j \leqslant \bar{z}\}$ is compact $\forall (c, \bar{z})$ in $R \times R^{S+1}_+$; $z^j_0 = 0$ implies $z^j = 0$; $\forall (y^j, z^j) \in Y^j$, there exists $(y^j, \tilde{z}^j) \in Y^j$ with $\tilde{z}^j_0 \leqslant z^j_0$, $\tilde{z}^j_s \leqslant k\tilde{z}^j_0$, $s = 1, \ldots, S$, $k < +\infty$; $\forall (y^j, 0) \in Y^j$, there exists $(\tilde{y}^j, \tilde{z}^j) \in Y^j$ with $\tilde{y}^j \geqslant y^j$.

The last two statements in assumption A.10, although introduced for technical convenience, reflect the idea that all labour contracts cover the two periods, and that labour is never totally unproductive.

For present purposes, the decisions of firms are split into (i) $d^j = (y^j, z^j_0)$, a decision about outputs in both periods y^j and about employment in period 0; that decision rests with the shareholders of the firm and is governed by the control principle; (ii) $c^j = (\rho^j, \tau^j)$, the terms of the labour contract, specifying for both periods the hours worked and the wages, *per unit of period 0 employment*; that decision is joint between shareholders and workers, and it is governed by the control principle with majority voting by workers.

In order to bring about (in the proof) equality of the demand and supply of labour, I replace τ^j_0 by a 'market' wage rate q^j and express the contractual wages (which are allowed to vary over time and across states) relatively to that market rate; accordingly, wages per unit of period 0 employment become $q_j\tau^j = (q_j, q_j\tau_1^j, \ldots, q_j\tau_S^j)$. Because the market wages are determined jointly with the stock prices p_j, $j = 1, \ldots, J$, and the price of the physical good p_0, the limited liability conditions for period 1 take the form

$$p_0 y_s^j - q_j \tau_s^j z_0^j \geqslant 0 \qquad s = 1, \ldots, S. \tag{A.13}$$

(This amounts to keeping the price level p_0 constant across time and states, and letting real wages $(q_j/p_0)\tau_s^j$ adjust freely.) Conditions (A.13) would become very restrictive at $p_0 = 0$, since they would impose $z_0^j = 0$, unless $q_j\tau_s^j = 0 \ \forall\, s = 1, \ldots, S$. I shall rely systematically on the quasi-equilibria approach and verify that $p_0 > 0$ at equilibrium.

Admissible contracts are defined by $c^j \in \mathscr{C}^j$, a compact convex subset of $R_+^{2(S+1)}$, such that $c^j \in \mathscr{C}^j$ implies $\rho_0^j \geqslant \rho_0 > 0$ and $\tau_0^j = 1$. That is, contracts are not allowed to stipulate wage adjustments (for overtime, seniority, profit-sharing, redundancy and so on) that deviate arbitrarily from market rates. And the status of 'employment in period 0' (which gives access to contractual rights) is predicated upon 'actual employment' (*not* working 0 hours). (The compactness requirement is a harmless matter of convenience.)

The set of feasible decisions for firm j thus depends upon c^j, q_j and p_0:

$$\begin{aligned} D^j(c^j, q_j, p_0) = \{y^j, z_0^j \mid (y^j, z_0^j \rho^j) \in Y^j, \\ p_0 y_s^j - q_j \tau_s^j z_0^j \geqslant 0, s = 1, \ldots, S\}. \end{aligned} \tag{A.14}$$

I note for further reference that, when $p_0 > 0$, one could write indifferently

$$\begin{aligned} D^j\left(c^j, \frac{q_j}{p_0}\right) = \Big\{ y^j, z_0^j \mid (y^j, z_0^j \rho^j) \in Y^j, \\ y_s^j - \frac{q_j}{p_0} \tau_s^j z_0^j \geqslant 0, s = 1, \ldots, S \Big\}. \end{aligned} \tag{A.15}$$

To simplify the proof, at no loss of generality, I shall also assume the following:

Assumption A.11

$\forall j$, $(y^j, z^j) \in Y^j$ implies $(\hat{y}^j + \lambda\eta, \hat{z}^j) \in Y^j \ \forall \lambda \geqslant 0$, $\hat{y}^j \leqslant y^j$ and $\hat{z}^j \geqslant z^j$, where $\eta = (-1, 1, \ldots, 1) \in R_- \times R_+^S$.

This combines free disposal, introduced through $\hat{y}^j$ and $\hat{z}^j$, with storability of output, introduced through η. In a single-commodity framework, storability at no cost is equivalent to non-negativity of the interest rate. (Assumption A.11 is used only once, to establish conveniently the continuity of $D^j(c^j, q_j, p_0)$, and could undoubtedly be relaxed.)

The I consumers, indexed $i = 1, \ldots, I$, have consumption sets $C^i \subset R_+^{2(S+1)}$, with elements (x^i, z^i) in $R_+^{S+1} \times R_+^{S+1}$, and initial endowments $w^i \in R_+^{S+1}$.

Assumption A.12

For each i, $C^i = R_+^{S+1} \times C_z^i$, where C_z^i is a compact convex subset of R_+^{S+1}, with $0 \in C_z^i$; $w^i \in \text{int } R_+^{S+1}$; the preference ordering $\succsim_i$ on C^i is continuous and convex; if $x^i \geqslant \tilde{x}^i$ and $z^i \leqslant \tilde{z}^i$, then $(x^i, z^i) \succsim_i (\tilde{x}^i, \tilde{z}^i)$; if in addition either $x_0^i > \tilde{x}_0^i$, or $z_0^i < \tilde{z}_0^i$, or $x_s^i > \tilde{x}_s^i \ \forall s = 1, \ldots, S$, or $z_s^i < \tilde{z}_s^i \ \forall\, s = 1, \ldots, S$, then $(x^i, z^i) \succ_i (\tilde{x}^i, \tilde{z}^i)$.

Shares of stock are still traded against commodity 0. It is now convenient to define a price vector as a pair (p,q) in $\Delta = \{(p,q) \in R_+^{2J+1} \mid \Sigma_{j=0}^J p_j + \Sigma_{j=1}^J q_j = 1\}$. Here, p_0 is the price of commodity 0, p_j is the price of firm j on the stock exchange, $j = 1, \ldots, J$, and $q_j \in R_+$ is the wage rate to be paid by firm j in period 0, $j = 1, \ldots, J$.

Initial and final holdings of shares of stock are still denoted by the matrices $\bar{\Theta}$ and Θ in $\mathcal{M}$.

Consumers choose a pair of vectors $(\theta_i, z_0^i) \in R_+^J \times R_+^J$, where θ_{ij} is the share of i in 'dividends' of the firm j and z_0^{ij} is the quantity of labour supplied by i to firm j in period 0. The resulting consumption and labour plan (x^i, z^i) of i is defined by:

$$z_0^i = \Sigma_j z_0^{ij}, \quad z_s^i = \Sigma_j z_0^{ij} \rho_s^j \quad s = 1, \ldots, S \tag{A.16}$$

$$p_0 x_0^i = p_0 w_0^i + \Sigma_j \bar{\theta}_{ij} p_j + \Sigma_j q_j z_0^{ij} + \Sigma_j \theta_{ij}(p_0 y_0^j - q_j z_0^j - p_j) \tag{A.17}$$

$$p_0 x_s^i = p_0 w_s^i + \Sigma_j q_j z_0^{ij} \tau_s^j + \Sigma_j \theta_{ij}(p_0 y_s^j - q_j z_0^j \tau_s^j) \quad s = 1, \ldots, S. \tag{A.18}$$

I shall write $(x^i, z^i)(\theta^i, z_0^i, p, q, c, d)$ for the pair of vectors defined by equalities (A.16)–(A.18); with the additional stipulation that $x_s^i = +\infty$, $s = 0, 1, \ldots, S$, when $p_0 = 0$. The set of feasible decisions for consumer i is

$$\begin{aligned} T_i(p,q,c,d) = \{(\theta^i, z_0^i) \in R_+^J \times R_+^J \mid \forall j,\ 1 \geq \theta_{ij} \geq 0, \\ \Sigma_j \theta_{ij}(p_j + q_j z_0^j - p_0 y_0^j) - \Sigma_j q_j z_0^{ij} \leq p_0 w_0^i + \Sigma_j \bar{\theta}_{ij} p_j, \\ z^i = (\Sigma_j z_0^{ij} \rho_0^j,\ \Sigma_j z_0^{ij} \rho_1^j, \ldots, \Sigma_j z_0^{ij} \rho_S^j) \in C_z^i\}. \end{aligned}$$

I shall write Z_0 for the matrix $[z_0^{ij}]$.

An *equilibrium of production, exchange and labour contracts* (or EPEC for definitions 3.1 and 3.2) is a tuple $(\Theta, Z_0, p, q, c, d)$ in $\mathcal{M} \times R_+^{IJ} \times \Delta \times C \times D$ specifying the portfolio and labour supply (θ^i, z_0^i) of each consumer i, a positive price level p_0 and the prices of the shares of stock and of the unit labour contracts of all firms (p, q), the terms $c^j = (\rho^j, \tau^j)$ of the labour contract and the production decision $d^j = (y^j, z_0^j)$ of each firm, and satisfying the following conditions:

(i) For each i, $(\theta^i, z_0^i) \in T^i(p,q,c,d)$, and there does not exist $(\hat{\theta}^i, \hat{z}_0^i) \in T^i(p,q,c,d)$ with

$$(x^i, z^i)(\hat{\theta}^i, \hat{z}_0^i, p, q, c, d) \succ_i (x^i, z^i)(\theta^i, z_0^i, p, q, c, d).$$

(ii) $(p,q) \in \Delta$, $\Theta \in \mathcal{M}$ and, for each j, $\Sigma_i z_0^{ij} = z_0^j$.

(iii) For each j, $d^j \in D^j(c^j, q_j, p_0)$ and there do not exist $\hat{d}^j \in D^j(c^j, q_j, p_0)$ and $\hat{\mathcal{I}}^j \in \{1, \ldots, I\}$ such that

$$\hat{\mathcal{I}}^j \supseteq \mathcal{I}^j(\Theta) \qquad \Sigma_i(\theta_{ij}: i \in \hat{\mathcal{I}}^j) > 1/2$$

and

$$(x^i + \theta_{ij}(\hat{y}^j - q_j \hat{z}_0^j \tau^j - y^j + q_j z_0^j \tau^j), z^i) \succ_i (x^i, z^i) \forall i \in \hat{\mathcal{I}}^j.$$

(iv) For each j, $c^j \in \mathcal{C}^j$ and there do not exist $\hat{c}^j \in \mathcal{C}^j$, $\hat{y}^j$ with $(\hat{y}^j, z_0^j) \in D^j(\hat{c}^j, q_j, p_0)$ and subsets $\hat{\mathcal{I}}^j, \tilde{\mathcal{I}}^j$ of $\{1, \ldots, I\}$ such that

(a) $\Sigma_i(z_0^{ij}: i \in \tilde{\mathcal{I}}^j) > (1/2)\, \Sigma_i z_0^{ij}$ and $\forall i \in \tilde{\mathcal{I}}^j$,

$$\left(x^i + z_0^{ij} \frac{q_j}{p_0}(\hat{\tau}^j - \tau^j), z^i + z_0^{ij}(\hat{\rho}^j - \rho^j)\right) \succ_i (x^i, z^i)$$

(b) $\mathcal{I}^j(\Theta) \subseteq \hat{\mathcal{I}}^j$, $\Sigma_i(\theta_{ij}: i \in \hat{\mathcal{I}}^j) > 1/2$ and $\forall i \in \hat{\mathcal{I}}^j$,

$$\left(x^i + \theta_{ij}\left(\hat{y}^j - \frac{q_j}{p_0}\hat{\tau}^j z_0^j - y^j + \frac{q_j}{p_0}\tau^j z_0^j\right), z^i\right) \succ_i (x^i, z^i).$$

Theorem 3.2

Under assumptions A.10–A.12 and CC′, there exists an EPEC for definitions 3.1 and 3.2.

Proof

The proof is a tedious[1] extension of that given above for theorem 2.2 in appendix 2, to which the reader is referred back for repetitious details. (Actually, theorem 2.2 is a special case of theorem 3.2, if one imposes $z_0^{ij} = z_0^j = 0 \ \forall \ i,j$.) I only write down the part of the proof establishing existence in the ϵ-economy.

The abstract economy now consists of $N = I + 2J + 1$ agents, with agents $1, \ldots, I + J$ corresponding again to consumers and firms, with the latter agents in charge of production decisions. Agent $I + J + k$ is in charge of the labour contract of firm k, $k = 1, \ldots, J$.

For consumer i, the choice set in the ϵ-economy is $X_i = \{(\theta^i, z_0^i) \mid \forall j, 1 \geqslant \theta_{ij} > \epsilon\hat{\theta}_{ij}; z_0^i \geqslant 0\}$; the constraint correspondence is

$$\mathscr{A}_i(x) = T_i^\epsilon(p,q,c,d) := T_i(p,q,c,d) \cap X_i$$

and the preference correspondence is

$$P_i(x) = \{\hat{\theta}^i, \hat{t}_0^i) \in X_i \mid (x^i, z^i)\ (\hat{\theta}^i, \hat{z}_0^i, p, q, c, d)$$
$$\succ_i (x^i, z^i)\ (\theta^i, z_0^i, p, q, c, d)\}.$$

For the J agents indexed $I + 1, \ldots, I + J$, in charge of the production decisions of the firms (reindexed $j = I + 1, \ldots, I + J$), the choice sets are

$$X_j = Y_d^j = \{(y^j, z_0^j) \mid \exists (\hat{y}^j, \hat{z}^j) \in Y^j, \hat{y}^j = y^j, \hat{z}_0^j = z_0^j\}.$$

The constraint correspondences are $\mathscr{A}_j(x) = D^j(c^j, q_j, p_0)$ and the preference correspondences are defined as follows. Let

$$\tilde{\theta}_{ij} = \frac{\theta_{ij}}{\Sigma_h \theta_{hj}} \qquad \tilde{d}^j = d^j \Sigma_h \theta_{hj} \qquad \tilde{\theta}^j = (\tilde{\theta}_{1j}, \ldots, \tilde{\theta}_{Ij}).$$

If $p_0 > 0$, then

$$P_j(x) = \{\hat{d}^j \in D^j(c^j, q_j, p_0) \mid \exists \hat{\mathscr{I}}^j \subseteq \{1, \ldots, I\}, \mathscr{I}^j(\tilde{\Theta}^j) \subseteq \hat{\mathscr{I}}^j,$$
$$\Sigma_i(\tilde{\theta}_{ij}: i \in \hat{\mathscr{I}}^j) > 1/2,$$
$$\left(x^i + \tilde{\theta}_{ij}\left(\hat{y}^j - \frac{q_j}{p_0}\hat{z}_0^j\tau^j - \tilde{y}^j + \frac{q^j}{p_0}\tilde{z}_0^j\tau^j\right), z^i\right)$$
$$\succ_i (x^i, z^i) \forall i \in \hat{\mathscr{I}}^j\}. \tag{A.19}$$

If $p_0 = 0$, then $P_j(x) = \phi$.

For the J agents indexed $I + J + 1, \ldots, I + 2J$, in charge of the labour contracts of the firms (reindexed $k = I + J + 1, \ldots, I + 2J$) the choice sets are $X_k = \mathscr{C}^k$, the constraint correspondences are $\mathscr{A}_k(x) = \mathscr{C}^k$, and the preference correspondences are defined as follows. Let

$$\tilde{\theta}_{ik} = \frac{\theta_{ik}}{\Sigma_h \theta_{hk}} \qquad \tilde{d}^k = d^k \Sigma_h \theta_{hk} \qquad \tilde{\theta}^k = (\tilde{\theta}_{hk}, \ldots, \tilde{\theta}_{Ik}).$$

If $p_0 > 0$, then

$$P_k(x) = \Big\{ (\hat{\rho}^k, \hat{\tau}^k) \in \mathscr{C}^k \,|\, \exists\, \hat{y}^k, (\hat{y}^k, z_0^k) \in D^k(\hat{c}^k, q_k, p_0);$$
$$\exists\, \tilde{\mathscr{I}}^k, \hat{\mathscr{I}}^k \text{ in } \{1, \ldots, I\}$$

such that

(i) $\Sigma_i(z_0^{ik} : i \in \tilde{\mathscr{I}}^k) > (1/2)\Sigma_i z_0^{ik}$ and $\forall\, i \in \tilde{\mathscr{I}}^k$,

$$\left(x^i + z_0^{ik} \frac{q_k}{p_0} (\hat{\tau}^k - \tau^k),\ z^i + z_0^{ik}(\hat{\rho}^k - \rho^k) \right) \succ_i (x^i, z^i) \tag{A.20}$$

(ii) $\mathscr{I}^k(\tilde{\Theta}) \subseteq \hat{\mathscr{I}}^k$, $\Sigma_i(\tilde{\theta}_{ik} : i \in \hat{\mathscr{I}}^k) > 1/2$ and $\forall\, i \in \hat{\mathscr{I}}^k$,

$$\left(x^i + \tilde{\theta}_{ik} \left(\hat{y}^k - \frac{q_k}{p_0} \tilde{z}_0^k \hat{\tau}^k - \tilde{y}^k + \frac{q_k}{p_0} \tilde{z}_0^k \tau^k \right), z^i \right) \succ_i (x^i, z^i) \Big\}$$

If $p_0 = 0$, then $P_k(x) = \phi$.

It follows from that definition that $P_k(x) = \phi\ \forall\, x$ with $\Sigma_i z_0^{ik} = 0$.

Agent $N = I + 2J + 1$ is the market agent with choice set $X_N = \Delta \subset R^{2J+1}$ of elements $(x_N =)\ (p, q)$, constraint correspondence $\mathscr{A}_N(x) \equiv \Delta$ and a preference correspondence defined by

$$P_N(x) = \{(\hat{p}, \hat{q}) \in \Delta \,|\, (\hat{p}_0 - p_0)(\Sigma_i x_0^i - \Sigma_{ij}\theta_{ij} y_0^j - \Sigma_i w_0^i) +$$
$$\Sigma_j(\hat{p}_j - p_j)(\Sigma_i \theta_{ij} - 1) +$$
$$\Sigma_j(\hat{q}_j - q_j)(\Sigma_i \theta_{ij} z_0^j - \Sigma_i z_0^{ij}) > 0\}. \tag{A.21}$$

To fit the economy so defined into the Shafer-Sonnenschein framework one notes that, for each $h = 1, \ldots, N$, X_h is a non-empty, closed and convex subset of R^l, where $l = 2IJ + 3(S+1)J + 2J + 1$ and R^l is the space of $(\Theta, Z_0, d, c, q, p)$. Standard techniques are applicable for bounding X_h, since $\Sigma_i w_0^i$ is finite, C_z^i is bounded for each i and the cut of each Y^j at finite (y_0^j, z^j) is bounded. Also, the bounds imply that $T_i^\epsilon(p, q, c, d) \neq \phi$ identically in (p, q, c, d) for ϵ small enough.

In so far as continuity of the constraint correspondences is concerned, the novelty (relative to the proof of theorem 2.2) comes from

$$D^j(c^j, q_j, p_0) = \{(y^j, z_0^j) \in Y_d^j \mid (y^j, z_0^j \rho^j) \in Y^j,\ p_0 y_s^j - q_j z_0^j \tau_s^j \geqslant 0\ \forall s = 1, \ldots, S\}.$$

Continuity of that correspondence for $p_0 > 0$ is readily verified through explicit consideration of sequences. Define, for the purposes of this specific argument, $\bar{q}_j = q_j / p_0$ and use (A.15). If, for all $\nu = 1, 2, \ldots, \infty$, $(\bar{q}_j^\nu, c^{j\nu}) \to (\bar{q}_j, c^j)$ and $d^{j\nu} \in D^j(\bar{q}_j^\nu, c^{j\nu})$ with $d^{j\nu} \to d^j$, then $d^j \in D^j(\bar{q}_j, c^j)$ because Y^j is closed, $z_0^{j\nu} \rho^{j\nu} \to z_0^j \rho^j$ and $y_s^j - \bar{q}_j z_0^j \tau_s^j \geqslant 0$ for all $s = 1, \ldots, S$; hence D^j is upper hemicontinuous. To establish lower hemicontinuity, let $(\bar{q}_j^\nu, c^{j\nu}) \to (\bar{q}_j, c^j)$ and let $(y^j, z_0^j) \in D^j(\bar{q}_j, c^j)$. To construct $(y^{j\nu}, z_0^{j\nu}) \in D^j(\bar{q}_j^\nu, c^{j\nu})$, $(y^{j\nu}, z_0^{j\nu}) \to (y^j, z_0^j)$, let $z_0^{j\nu} = \operatorname{argmin} \{z_0^{j\nu} \mid \ell_s^{j\nu} \geqslant z_0^j \rho_s^j\ \forall s = 0, 1, \ldots, S\}$ and $y^{j\nu} = y^j + \lambda^\nu \eta$, with $\lambda^\nu = \operatorname{argmin} \{\lambda^\nu \geqslant 0 \mid y_s^j + \lambda^\nu \geqslant \bar{q}_j^\nu z_0^{j\nu} \tau_s^{j\nu}\ \forall s = 1, \ldots, S\}$. (Note that $\rho_s^{j\nu} = 0$ along a subsequence would imply $\rho_s^j = 0$, imposing no constraint on $z_0^{j\nu}$.) Then $(y^{j\nu}, z_0^{j\nu} \rho^{j\nu}) \in Y^j$ by assumption A.11, $y_s^{j\nu} - \bar{q}_j^\nu z_0^{j\nu} \tau_s^{j\nu} \geqslant 0$ by construction, $s = 1, \ldots, S$; and $z_0^{j\nu} \to z_0^j$, $\lambda^\nu \to 0$ since $z_0^{j\nu} = z_0^j \rho_s^j / \rho_s^{j\nu}$ for some s and either $\lambda^\nu = 0$ or $-\lambda^\nu = y_s^j - \bar{q}_j z_0^j \tau_s^j + (\bar{q}_j z_0^j \tau_s^j - \bar{q}_j^\nu z_0^{j\nu} \tau_s^{j\nu}) < 0$ for some s, with $y_s^j - \bar{q}_j z_0^j \tau_s^j \geqslant 0$ and $\bar{q}_j z_0^j \tau_s^j - \bar{q}_j^\nu z_0^{j\nu} \tau_s^{j\nu} \to 0$. For $p_0 = 0$, use the technique of quasi-equilibria.

The constraint correspondences of the remaining agents are constant. That $\mathscr{A}_i(x)$ is non-empty and convex for all i and x is readily verified.

The preference correspondences have open graph, and verify the condition that x_i does not belong to the convex hull of $P_i(x)$. The line of reasoning in the proof of theorem 2.2 remains applicable here. In particular, it is now the case that (A.16)–(A.18) are linear in (θ_i, z_0^i) and the preferences of the consumers are still continuous convex. In so far as the firms are concerned, the line of reasoning in the proof of theorem 2.2 remains valid, step by step. Indeed, when $p_0 \neq 0$, x_i is a continuous function of all its arguments; and when $p_0 = 0$, $P_j(x) = \phi$, $j = I+1, \ldots, I+J$. For the labour contracts, that is for $k = I+J+1, \ldots, I+2J$, the definition (A.7)′ is readily extended to

$$P_k(x) = \operatorname{def} P_k^*(x) \cap \operatorname{comp} P_k^o(x) \cap \operatorname{comp} P_k^{oo}(x), \qquad \text{(A.20)}'$$

where: $P_k^*(x)$ denotes as before the intersection of the preferred sets of the members of the control group; $P_k^o(x)$ denotes the union of intersections of preferred-or-indifferent sets over groups of shareholders holding at least half the shares; and $P_k^{oo}(x)$ denotes a similar construction for workers. To verify that (ρ^k, τ^k) does not belong to the convex hull of $P_k(x)$, it suffices to verify that it does not belong to $P_k^*(x)$, a convex set because shareholders' preferences over (ρ^k, τ^k) pairs are convex. If $(\hat{\rho}^k, \hat{\tau}^k)$ and $(\bar{\rho}^k, \bar{\tau}^k)$ both belong to $P_k^*(x)$ and $\mu \in [0,1]$, then $(\mu\hat{\rho}^k + (1-\mu)\bar{\rho}^k, \mu\hat{\tau}^k + (1-\mu)\bar{\tau}^k)$ also belongs to $P_k^*(x)$. Indeed, $(\mu\hat{y}^k + (1-\mu)\bar{y}^k, \mu z_0^k\hat{\rho}^k + (1-\mu)z_0^k\bar{\rho}^k)$ belongs to Y^k,

$$p_0[\mu\hat{y}_s^k + (1-\mu)\bar{y}_s^k] - z_0^k q_k[\mu\hat{\tau}^k + (1-\mu)\hat{\tau}_s^k] \geqslant 0 \qquad s = 1, \ldots, S,$$

and

$$x^i + \tilde{\theta}_{ik}\left[\mu\left(\hat{y}^k - \frac{q_k}{p_0}\tilde{z}_0^k\hat{\tau}^k\right) + (1-\mu)\left(\bar{y}^k - \frac{q_k}{p_0}\tilde{z}_0^k\bar{\tau}^k\right) - \tilde{y}^k + \frac{q_k}{p_0}\tilde{z}_0^k\tau^k\right]$$

$$= \mu\left[x^i + \tilde{\theta}_{ik}\left(\hat{y}^k - \frac{q_k}{p_0}\tilde{z}_0^k\hat{\tau}^k - \tilde{y}^k + \frac{q_k}{p_0}\tilde{z}_0^k\tau^k\right)\right] + (1-\mu)\left[x^i + \tilde{\theta}_{ik}\left(\bar{y}^k - \frac{q_k}{p_0}\tilde{z}_0^k\bar{\tau}^k - \tilde{y}^k + \frac{q_k}{p_0}\tilde{z}_0^k\tau^k\right)\right].$$

The line of reasoning in the proof of theorem 2.2, to the effect that $P_j(x)$ as defined in (A.7)′ has open graph, applies to $P_k(x)$ as defined in (A.20)′. Indeed, when $p_0 \neq 0$, (x^i, z^i) are continuous functions of all their arguments; and when $p_0 = 0$, $P_k(x) = \phi$.

Thus the Shafer-Sonnenschein-Greenberg theorem holds, and there exists a tuple $(\Theta, Z_0, p, q, c, d)$ such that, for each $i = 1, \ldots, N$, $x_i \in \mathscr{A}_i(x)$, and $P_i(x) \cap \mathscr{A}_i(x) = \phi$ provided $p_0 > 0$.

That $p_0 > 0$ is now verified as follows. The argument in the proof of theorem 2.2 now implies $p_0 + \Sigma_j q_j > 0$. If $p_0 = 0$, then $\Sigma_i x_0^i - \Sigma_{ij}\theta_{ij}y_0^j - \Sigma_i w_0^i$ is a large positive number – say M. In order for $P_N(x)$ to be empty, it must then be the case that $\Sigma_j q_j = 1$ with $\Sigma_i \theta_{ij} z_0^j - \Sigma_i z_0^{ij} = M$ for each j with $q_j > 0$. Indeed, $P_N = \phi$ with $p_0 = 0$ implies that the argument of every positive variable p_j or q_j be at least equal to M – which is not possible for p_j. Thus there exist a set of firms $\hat{J}$ such that $\Sigma_{j \in \hat{J}} q_j = 1$ and $\Sigma_i \theta_{ij} z_0^j - \Sigma_i z_0^{ij} = M \; \forall j \in \hat{J}$. But that in turn is impossible. Indeed, summing the equalities (A.17) and using $p_j = 0 \; \forall j$, we obtain

$$\Sigma_j q_j(\Sigma_i \theta_{ij} z_0^j - \Sigma_i z_0^{ij}) = 0$$

a contradiction. Therefore $p_0 > 0$, and every quasi-equilibrium is an equilibrium.

Let then

$$\Sigma_i x_0^i - \Sigma_{ij}\theta_{ij}y_0^j - \Sigma_i w_0^i = \text{def } \delta_0.$$

It must then be the case, either that $\delta_0 = 0$ or that $\delta_0 \geqslant 0$ and the argument of every other non-zero variable p_j or q_j is also equal to δ_0. Actually, we must have $\delta_0 = 0$, for otherwise, by $P_N(x) = \phi$,

$$p_0\delta_0 + \Sigma_j p_j(\Sigma_i\theta_{ij} - 1) + \Sigma_j q_j(\Sigma_i\theta_{ij}z_0^j - \Sigma_i z_0^{ij}) = \delta_0$$

whereas, summing the budget constraints (A.17) which hold as equalities,

$$p_0\delta_0 + \Sigma_j p_j(\Sigma_i\theta_{ij} - 1) + \Sigma_j q_j(\Sigma_i\theta_{ij}z_0^j - \Sigma_i z_0^{ij}) = 0.$$

Thus $\delta_0 = 0$.

It then immediately follows that $q_j > 0$ and $\Sigma_i\theta_{ij}z_0^j - \Sigma_i z_0^{ij} = 0$, for all j. Indeed, $q_j = 0$ would, by assumptions A.10 and A.12, imply $z_0^j > 0$, $z_0^{ij} = 0$; in which case, $\hat{q}_0^j = 1$ would contradict $P_N(x) = \phi$.

Finally, for each j, either $\Sigma_i\theta_{ij} - 1 = 0$, or $p_j = 0$ with $\Sigma_i\theta_{ij} < 1$; hence $\Sigma_i\tilde{\theta}_{ij} = 1$ as desired.

That conditions (i), (ii), (iii) and (iv) in the definition of an EPEC are all verified is immediate, following the line of reasoning in the proof of theorem 2.2. □

Note

1 In such a tedious exercise, the probability that I overlooked some technical detail is quite high; but I am confident that technical adjustments in the assumptions would take care of such details. I am not interested here in minimality of technical assumptions.

Appendix 4

In this appendix I spell out the properties of Pareto-efficient contracts, which are discussed in section 3.4. To facilitate the analysis, I assume that the production set Y^j is representable by a continuously differentiable function, which may be taken as giving spot investment y^j_0 as a function of the state distribution of outputs and of all labour inputs:

$$y^j_0 = f^j(y^j_1, \ldots, y^j_S, z^j_0, z^j_1, \ldots, z^j_S). \tag{A.22}$$

Needless to say, the differentiability assumption is rather extreme, in the present context where joint production across states is apt to be the rule rather than the exception. With convex production sets, however, the assumption is still useful because it helps to bring out conveniently, in terms of derivatives, properties that hold more generally in terms of subdifferentials or elements of normal cones.

The model of this appendix rests on the definition of consumption-and-labour plans in (3.2)–(3.4), reproduced and renumbered here for convenience:

$$x^i_0 = w^i_0 + \Sigma_j \bar{\theta}_{ij} p_j + \Sigma_j \zeta_{ij} t^j_0 + \Sigma_j \theta_{ij}(y^j_0 - t^j_0 - p_j) \tag{A.23}$$

$$x^i_s = w^i_s + \Sigma_j \zeta_{ij} t^j_s + \Sigma_j \theta_{ij}(y^j_s - t^j_s) \tag{A.24}$$

$$z^i = \Sigma_j \zeta_{ij} z^j. \tag{A.25}$$

The problem of defining Pareto-optimal decisions by the firms, for given portfolios (θ_i, ζ_i) of the consumers, can be stated as follows (with undetermined positive parameters λ^i):

$$\max_{(y^j, z^j, t^j)(j=1, \ldots, J)} \Lambda = \Sigma_i \lambda^i u^i(x^i, z^i)$$

subject to (A.22)–(A.25). (A.26)

The first-order conditions for problem (A.26) are

$$\frac{\partial \Lambda}{\partial t_0^j} = \Sigma_i \lambda^i \frac{\partial u^i}{\partial x_0^i} (\zeta_{ij} - \theta_{ij}) = 0 \tag{A.27}$$

$$\frac{\partial \Lambda}{\partial t_s^j} = \Sigma_i \lambda^i \frac{\partial u^i}{\partial x_s^i} (\zeta_{ij} - \theta_{ij}) = 0 \tag{A.28}$$

$$\frac{\partial \Lambda}{\partial z_0^j} = \Sigma_i \lambda^i \left[\frac{\partial u^i}{\partial x_0^i} \theta_{ij} \frac{\partial y_0^j}{\partial z_0^j} + \frac{\partial u^i}{\partial z_0^i} \zeta_{ij} \right] = 0 \tag{A.29}$$

$$\frac{\partial \Lambda}{\partial z_s^j} = \Sigma_i \lambda^i \left[\frac{\partial u^i}{\partial x_0^i} \theta_{ij} \frac{\partial y_0^j}{\partial z_s^j} + \frac{\partial u^i}{\partial z_s^i} \zeta_{ij} \right] = 0 \tag{A.30}$$

$$\frac{\partial \Lambda}{\partial y_s^j} = \Sigma_i \lambda^i \left[\frac{\partial u^i}{\partial x_0^i} \theta_{ij} \frac{\partial y_0^j}{\partial y_s^j} + \frac{\partial u^i}{\partial x_s^i} \theta_{ij} \right] = 0. \tag{A.31}$$

Defining

$$\mu^i = \lambda^i \frac{\partial u^i}{\partial x_0^i} \qquad \pi_s^i = \frac{\partial u^i}{\partial x_s^i} \Big/ \frac{\partial u^i}{\partial x_0^i} \qquad \gamma_s^j = -\frac{\partial y_0^j}{\partial y_s^j}$$
$$\frac{dx_s^i}{dz_s^i} = -\frac{\partial u^i}{\partial z_s^i} \Big/ \frac{\partial u^i}{\partial x_s^i} \tag{A.32}$$

we may rewrite these conditions as follows:

$$\Sigma_i \mu^i \zeta_{ij} = \Sigma_i \mu^i \theta_{ij} = 1 \tag{A.33}$$

$$\Sigma_i \mu^i \zeta_{ij} \pi_s^i = \Sigma_i \mu^i \theta_{ij} \pi_s^i \tag{A.34}$$

$$\frac{\partial y_0^j}{\partial z_0^j} = \Sigma_i \mu^i \zeta_{ij} \frac{dx_0^i}{dz_0^i} \tag{A.35}$$

$$\frac{\partial y_0^j}{\partial z_s^j} = \Sigma_i \mu^i \zeta_{ij} \pi_s^i \frac{dx_s^i}{dz_s^i} \tag{A.36}$$

$$\gamma_s^j = \Sigma_i \mu_i \theta_{ij} \pi_s^i. \tag{A.37}$$

Equalities (A.34), (A.36) and (A.37) together also imply:

$$\frac{dy_s^j}{dz_s^j} = \Sigma_i \mu^i \zeta_{ij} \pi_s^i \frac{dx_s^i/dz_s^i}{\Sigma_i \mu^i \zeta_{ij} \pi_s^i}$$
$$= \Sigma_i \mu^i \zeta_{ij} \frac{dx_s^i}{dz_s^i} \left[1 + \frac{\text{cov}(\pi_s^i, dx_s^i/dz_s^i)}{(\Sigma_i \mu^i \zeta_{ij} \pi_s^i)(\Sigma_i \mu^i \zeta_{ij}\, dx_s^i/dz_s^i)} \right] \tag{A.38}$$

The covariance in (A.38) is evaluated across *individuals* (with weights $\mu^i \zeta_{ij}$), not across states; accordingly, no statement about its sign is possible on *a priori* grounds.

Appendix 5

In order to investigate some of the issues raised in chapter 5, I use a variant of the highly streamlined model introduced in the appendix of Drèze (1986) and extended in Gollier (1988).

The physical model is one where aggregate production *tomorrow* is constrained by a state-dependent neoclassical production function relating output Y_s to labour input L_s in every state s:

$$Y_s = f_s(L_s) \qquad f_s'(L_s) > 0 \qquad f_s''(L_s) < 0 \qquad s = 1, \ldots, S. \tag{A.39}$$

Thus the stock of capital available for use tomorrow is taken as given (predetermined), and is therefore not mentioned explicitly. The labour input is split between L_0 workers under contract (insiders), who are assumed to be employed in all states, and $L_s \leqslant L$ workers of a new generation, who are assumed to supply inelastically one unit of labour each. (L is the size of the new generation.) Thus the utility of leisure is ignored (for instance, on the grounds that it is offset by the positive value of having a job; more realistic specifications are possible, but introduce unnecessary complications). The wage paid to workers under contract is w_{0s}, that specified in a new contract is w_s, and the cardinal (von Neumann-Morgenstern) utility function for income of a worker (of either generation) is denoted $u(y)$; it is assumed to be strictly concave (risk aversion) and twice continuously differentiable:

$$u = u(y) \qquad u'(y) > 0 \qquad u''(y) < 0. \tag{A.40}$$

Output price is normalized to unity in every state. Hence profits associated with the employment of newcomers are simply (subsuming L_0 under f_s)

$$\hat{\pi}_s = f_s(L_s) - w_{0s}L_0 - w_sL_s \qquad s = 1, \ldots, S. \tag{A.41}$$

I assume that firms maximize these profits *ex post* in every state, by choosing L_s while taking wages as given. This calls for equating the wage rate to the marginal (value) product of labour:

$$f_s'(L_s) = w_s \qquad s = 1, \ldots, S. \tag{A.42}$$

I shall denote by $L_s(w_s)$ the labour demand function implicitly defined by (A.42). It satisfies

$$L_s'(w_s) = \frac{1}{f_s''(L_s)} < 0 \qquad \eta_{L_s w_s} := \eta_s = \frac{w_s L_s'}{L_s} = \frac{f_s'(L_s)}{L_s f_s''(L_s)} < 0 \tag{A.43}$$

where η_s denotes the wage elasticity of *new hirings* (*not* of total employment).

I assume that profit earners hold market portfolios, and that their preferences can be represented by an aggregate utility function V, with argument profits minus taxes. The latter are simply a lump-sum tax on profits, used to finance a scheme of unemployment benefits, in an amount t_s per unemployed person. The after-tax profits are thus $\hat{\pi}_s - t_s(L - L_s) = \text{def } \pi_s$.

The characterization of *ex ante* Pareto-efficient transfer-and-wage policies is obtained from the first-order conditions for maximizing a weighted sum of expected utilities, namely that of profit earners (a function of their net profits) with weight λ and that of workers with weight unity, where the expected utility of a worker is computed with probabilities of employment and unemployment equal to L_s/L and $(L - L_s)/L$ respectively. The weight λ reflects distributive ethics.

It is assumed that all agents agree about the probabilities of the states, $\phi_s > 0, s = 1, \ldots, S$. Expectations in terms of these probabilities are denoted E_s. Finally, it is assumed that $u'(y) \to +\infty$ as $y \to 0$, so that the conditions $(L - L_s)t_s \geqslant 0$ are never binding (for t_s); and that $f_s'(L_s)$ is high enough so that the conditions $L_s \geqslant 0$ are never binding.

These specifications lead to the following problem:

$$\max_{w_{0s}, w_s, t_s} \Lambda = \lambda E_s V[f_s(L_s) - w_{0s}L_0 - w_sL_s - t_s(L - L_s)] \tag{A.44}$$
$$+ E_s \left\{ L_0 u(w_{0s}) + L \left[\frac{L_s}{L} u(w_s) + \frac{L - L_s}{L} u(t_s) \right] \right\}$$

subject to (A.42) and to

$$w_{0s} \geqslant w_s \quad (\rho_s)$$

$$w_s \geqslant t_s \quad (\mu_s)$$

$$L \geqslant L_s \quad (\nu_s)$$

where ρ_s, μ_s and ν_s are Lagrange multipliers.

The condition $w_s \geqslant t_s$ is introduced to guarantee that workers will accept employment at the wage w_s. (The implicit rate of income taxation should not exceed 100 per cent). The condition $w_{0s} \geqslant w_s$ is a standard requirement (of incentive compatibility).

The first-order necessary conditions for this problem are:

$$\frac{\partial \Lambda}{\partial w_{0s}} = -\lambda\phi_s V'(\pi_s)L_0 + \phi_s u'(w_{0s})L_0 + \rho_s = 0 \tag{A.45}$$

$$\frac{\partial \Lambda}{\partial w_s} = -\lambda\phi_s V'(\pi_s)[L_s - t_s L_s'(w_s)] + \phi_s[L_s u'(w_s) + L_s'(w_s)\{u(w_s) - u(t_s)\}] + \mu_s - \nu_s L'(w_s) - \rho_s = 0 \tag{A.46}$$

$$\frac{\partial \Lambda}{\partial t_s} = -\lambda\phi_s V'(\pi_s)(L - L_s) + \phi_s u'(t_s)(L - L_s) - \mu_s = 0. \tag{A.47}$$

In order to analyse these conditions, I first show that (i) $L = L_s$ implies $\mu_s = 0$, and (ii) $L > L_s$ implies $\mu_s > 0$. I will next show that (iii) $\mu_s > 0$ implies $w_{0s} > w_s$ and $\rho_s = 0$.

Property (i) follows immediately from (A.47).

To establish property (ii), I note that $L > L_s$ with $\mu_s = 0$ would imply through (A.47) that $u'(t_s) = \lambda V'(\pi_s)$. Also, $L > L_s$ implies $\nu_s = 0$. Using these two properties, (A.46) could be solved for

$$\frac{\rho_s}{\phi_s} = u'(t_s)t_s L_s'(w_s) + L_s[u'(w_s) - u'(t_s)] + L_s'(w_s)[u(w_s) - u(t_s)] < 0, \tag{A.48}$$

contradicting $\rho_s \geqslant 0$; where the negative sign in (A.48) follows from $L_s' < 0$ and $w_s \geqslant t_s$. Hence $L > L_s$ implies $\mu_s > 0$.

To establish property (iii), I note that $\mu_s > 0$ and $w_{0s} = w_s$ would imply $w_{0s} = w_s = t_s$ with $L > L_s$. It would then follow from (A.45) that $\lambda V'(\pi_s) - u'(t_s) = \rho_s/\phi_S L_0 \geqslant 0$, and from (A.47) that $\lambda V'(\pi_s) - u'(t_s) = -\mu_s/\phi_s(L - L_s) < 0$, a contradiction. Hence $\mu_s > 0$ implies $w_{0s} > w_s$ and $\rho_s = 0$.

Using these properties, and noting that t_s is irrelevant when $L = L_s$, we may confine the analysis to three cases:

(a) $L = L_s$ with $w_{0s} = w_s$
(b) $L = L_s$ with $w_{0s} > w_s$
(c) $L > L_s$ with $w_{0s} > w_s = t_s$.

The relevant characteristics for these three cases go as follows.

First, $L = L_s$ means that $w_s = f_s'(L) := w_s^*$, where w_s^* denotes the market-clearing wage; and $L > L_s$ means that $w_s > w_s^*$.

Second, when $w_{0s} > w_s$ so that $\rho_s = 0$, it follows from (A.45) that

$$u'(w_{0s}) = \lambda V'(\pi_s), \tag{A.49}$$

namely the condition for optimal sharing (of income and risks) between workers under contract and property owners. On the other hand, when $\rho_s > 0$, then $u'(w_{0s}) = \lambda V'(\pi_s) - (\rho_s/\phi_s L_0) < \lambda V'(\pi_s)$, and wages exceed the level desired on distributive grounds.

Third, when $L > L_s$ so that $\mu_s > 0, \rho_s = \nu_s = 0$, and $w_{0s} > w_s = t_s > w_s^*$, then (A.45)–(A.47) imply

$$\begin{aligned} u'(w_s) = u'(t_s) &= \lambda V'(\pi_s) \left[1 - \frac{w_s}{L} L_s'(w_s) \right] \\ &= \lambda V'(\pi_s) \left(1 - \frac{L_s}{L} \eta_s \right) \qquad \text{(A.50)} \\ &= u'(w_{0s}) \left(1 - \frac{L_s}{L} \eta_s \right). \end{aligned}$$

Condition (A.50) implies that unemployment sets in when $u'(w_s^*) = u'(w_{0s})(1 - \eta_s)$, that is when the market-clearing wage w_s^* carries a marginal utility exceeding that of the contractual wage w_{0s} by a percentage equal to $-100\ \eta_s$ (per cent).

One way to interpret (A.50) is as follows: raising $w_s(= t_s)$ yields additional utility to workers, evaluated as $Lu'(w_s)$; the cost to property owners is the higher level of payments to labour – either as wages or as unemployment benefits financed by the tax – plus the loss of output due to the reduced employment, a loss measured by $f_s'(L_s)\, L_s'(w_s) = w_s L_s'(w_s) = L_s \eta_s$. Hence the first-order condition:

$$Lu'(w_s) = \lambda V'(\pi_s)\,[L - w_s L_s'(w_s)]. \tag{A.50$'$}$$

To sum up, a solution to problem (A.44), defining *ex ante efficient* wage and unemployment benefits, can take either one of three forms, depending upon the position of the technological frontier $f_s(L_s)$ and hence upon the level of the full employment wages:

(a) $w_s = w_s^* = w_{0s} \qquad u'(w_{0s}) \leqslant \lambda V'(\pi_s).$

There is full employment, wages of the two generations of workers are both equal to the marginal value product of labour, and (possibly) higher than the level corresponding to optimal risk-sharing between workers under contract and property owners.

(b) $w_s = w_s^* < w_{0s} \qquad u'(w_{0s}) = \lambda V'(\pi_s) \qquad u'(w_s) \leqslant u'(w_{0s})(1 - \eta_s).$

There is full employment, but the wages of the two generations of workers are different (though not too different), those of the workers under contract being higher than the marginal value product of labour thanks to the income insurance supplied by property owners (against lower wages in the earlier periods).

(c) $w_{0s} > w_s = t_s > w_s^* \qquad L_s < L$

$$u'(w_s) = u'(w_{0s})\left(1 - \frac{L_s}{L}\eta_s\right) = \lambda V'(\pi_s) \left(1 - \frac{L_s}{L}\eta_s\right).$$

There is less than full employment, the wages of the two generations are different, with those of the older generation exceeding the marginal value product of labour, those of the younger generation equal to that marginal product and equal to the level of the unemployment benefits; thus all the unemployment is voluntary.

These conclusions may also be put in more sanguine terms as follows: all unemployment is voluntary and necessarily accompanied by wage discrimination between the two generations.

The fact that unemployment is voluntary is a consequence of allowing $t_s = w_s$. If one imposed instead, for incentive reasons, that $t_s \leqslant \alpha w_s$, $\alpha < 1$, then unemployment would be voluntary *ex ante* for workers as a group, but involuntary *ex post* for unemployed individuals.

The practical implications of conditions (A.50) are most conveniently explored by means of the linear approximation

$$
\begin{aligned}
u'(w_s) &= u'(w_{0s}) + (w_s - w_{0s})u''(w_{0s}) \\
&= u'(w_{0s})\left\{1 + (w_{0s} - w_s)\left[-\frac{u''(w_{0s})}{u'(w_{0s})}\right]\right\} \\
&= u'(w_{0s})[1 + (w_{0s} - w_s)R_A(w_{0s})] \\
&= u'(w_{0s})\left[1 + \frac{w_{0s} - w_s}{w_{0s}} R_R(w_{0s})\right]
\end{aligned}
\tag{A.51}
$$

where $R_A(w_{0s})$ and $R_R(w_{0s})$ are respectively the absolute and relative risk-aversion measures of Arrow (1965) and Pratt (1964) evaluated at w_{0s}. Inserting (A.51) into (A.50) yields

$$
\frac{w_{0s} - w_s}{w_{0s}} = \frac{-(L_s/L)\eta_s}{R_R(w_{0s})} \geqslant 0 \qquad w_s = w_{0s}\left[1 + \frac{(L_s/L)\eta_s}{R_R(w_{0s})}\right]. \tag{A.52}
$$

Thus the margin of relative discrimination $(w_{0s} - w_s)/w_{0s}$ is inversely proportional to the relative risk aversion of the workers, and directly proportional to the absolute value of the wage elasticity of new hirings. These two properties are intuitively natural.

References

Allais, M. 1953: L'extension des théories de l'équilibre économique général et du rendement social au cas du risque. *Econometrica*, 21, 269–90.

Armstrong, P.J. 1984: *Technical Change and Reduction in Life Hours of Work*. London: Technical Change Centre.

Arrow, K.J. 1953: Le rôle des valeurs boursières pour la répartition la meilleure des risques. *Económétrie*, Colloque International XL, Paris, CNRS, 41–47; translated as 'The role of securities in the optimal allocation of risk-bearing', *Review of Economics Studies*, 1964, 31, 91–96.

Arrow, K.J. 1965: *Aspects of the Theory of Risk-Bearing*. Helsinki: Yrjö Jahnsson Foundation.

Arrow, K.J. 1970a: *Essays in the Theory of Risk-Bearing*. Amsterdam: North-Holland.

Arrow, K.J. 1970b: Optimal insurance policies, pp. 212–19 in Arrow (1970a).

Azariadis, C. 1975: Implicit contracts and underemployment equilibria. *Journal of Political Economy*, 83, 1183–1202.

Azariadis, C. 1983: Employment with asymmetric information. *Quarterly Journal of Economics* (supplement), 83, 1183–1202.

Baily, M. 1974: Wages and employment under uncertain demand. *Review of Economic Studies*, 41, 37–50.

Bartlett, W. and Uvalic, M. 1985: Bibliography on labour-managed firms and employee participation. EUI Working Paper 85/198, Badia Fiesolana, San Domenico (FI).

Baudier, E. 1959: L'introduction du temps dans la théorie de l'équilibre général. *Cahiers Economiques*, 9–16.

Baumol, W.J.; Panzar, J.C. and Willig, R.D. 1982: *Contestable Markets and the Theory of Industry Structure*. New York: Harcourt Brace Jovanovich.

Becker, G. 1964: *Human Capital: a theoretical and empirical analysis with special reference to education*. New York: Columbia University Press.

Borch, K. 1960: The safety loading of reinsurance premiums. *Skandinavisk Aktuarietidskrift*, 43, 163–84.

Borch, K. 1962: Equilibrium in a reinsurance market. *Econometrica*, 30, 3, 424–44.

Debreu, G. 1959: *Theory of Value*. New York: Wiley.

Defourny, J. 1982: The problem of self-financing in workers cooperatives: a survey. Université de Liège and CIRIEC, 82/03.

Diamond, P.A. 1967: The role of a stock market in a general equilibrium model with technological uncertainty. *American Economic Review*, 57, 759–76.

Domar, E. 1966: The Soviet collective farm as a producer cooperative. *American Economic Review*, 56, 4, 737–57.

Drèze, J.H. 1971: Market allocation under uncertainty. *European Economic Review*, 2, 133–65; chapter 6 in Drèze (1987a).

Drèze, J.H. 1974a: *Allocation under Uncertainty: equilibrium and optimality*. Proceedings of an International Economic Association Conference (ed. J.H. Drèze), London: Macmillan.

Drèze, J.H. 1974b: Investment under private ownership: optimality, equilibrium and stability. Chapter 9 in Drèze (1974a); chapter 14 in Drèze (1987a).

Drèze, J.H. 1974c: The pure theory of labour-managed and participatory economies, part I: certainty. CORE DP 7422, Louvain-la-Neuve: Université Catholique de Louvain.

Drèze, J.H. 1975: Existence of an exchange equilibrium under price rigidities. *International Economic Review*, 16, 2, 301–20.

Drèze, J.H. 1976: Some theory of labour management and participation. *Econometrica*, 44, 6, 1125–39; chapter 18 in Drèze (1987a).

Drèze, J.H. 1979: Human capital and risk-bearing. *The Geneva Papers on Risk and Insurance*, 12, 5–22; chapter 17 in Drèze (1987a).

Drèze, J.H. 1981: Inferring risk tolerance from deductibles in insurance contracts. *The Geneva Papers on Risk and Insurance*, 20, 48–52; chapter 5 in Drèze (1987a).

Drèze, J.H. 1982: Decision criteria for business firms. In M. Hazewinkel and A.H.G. Rinnooy Kan (eds), *Current Developments in the Interface: economics, econometrics, mathematics*, Dordrecht: D. Reidel, 27–51; chapter 15 in Drèze (1987a).

Drèze, J.H. 1984: Autogestion et équilibre général. *Revue Européenne des Sciences Sociales*, 22, 66, 208–29.

Drèze, J.H. 1985a: Labour management and general equilibrium. In *Advances in the Economic Analysis of Participatory and Labour-Managed Firms*, JAI Press, 1, 3–20.

Drèze, J.H. 1985b: (Uncertainty and) the firm in general equilibrium theory. *Economic Journal*, 95 (supplement: conference papers), 1–20; chapter 16 in Drèze (1987a).

Drèze, J.H. 1985c: Second-best analysis with markets in disequilibrium: public sector pricing in a Keynesian regime. *European Economic Review*, 29, 263–301.

Drèze, J.H. 1986: Work-sharing: some theory and recent European experience. *Economic Policy*, 1, 3, 561–620.

Drèze, J.H. 1987a: *Essays on Economic Decisions under Uncertainty*. Cambridge: Cambridge University Press.

Drèze, J.H. 1987b: Underemployment equilibria: from theory to econometrics and policy. *European Economic Review*, 31, 9–34.

Drèze, J.H. and de la Vallée Poussin, D. 1971: A tâtonnement process for public goods. *The Review of Economic Studies*, 38, 2, 133–50.

Drèze, J.H. and Greenberg, J. 1980: Hedonic coalitions: optimality and stability. *Econometrica*, 48, 4, 987–1003.

Drèze, J.H. and Hagen, K. 1978: Choice of product quality: equilibrium and efficiency. *Econometrica*, 46, 3, 493–513.

Drèze, J.H. and Modigliani, F. 1972: Consumption decisions under uncertainty. *Journal of Economic Theory*, 5, 3, 308–35; chapter 9 in Drèze (1987a).

Drèze, J.H. and Modigliani, F. 1981: The trade-off between real wages and employment in an open economy (Belgium). *The European Economic Review*, 15, 1–40.

Emerson, M. 1988: *What Model for Europe*. Cambridge, Mass.: MIT Press.

Estrin, S. 1981: Income dispersion in a self-managed economy. *Economica*, 48, 181–94.

Estrin, S. and Svejnar, J. 1982: Wage determination under labour management: theory and evidence from Yugoslavia. Working Paper 192, Cornell University.

Furubotn, E.G. and Pejovich, S. 1973: Property rights and the behaviour of the firm in a socialist state: the example of Yugoslavia. *Zeitschrift für Nationalökonomie*, 30, 3–4, 431–54.

Geanakoplos, J. and Ito, T. 1982: On implicit contracts and involuntary unemployment. Cowles Foundations Discussion Paper 640, Yale University.

Geanakoplos, J., Magill, M., Quinzii, M. and Drèze, J.H. 1987: Generic inefficiency of stock-market equilibrium when markets are incomplete. *Journal of Mathematical Economics*, forthcoming.

Gevers, L. 1974: Competitive equilibrium of the stock exchange and Pareto efficiency. Chapter 10 in Drèze (1974a).

Gollier, C. 1988: *Intergenerational Risk-Sharing and Unemployment*. Unpublished PhD dissertation, Louvain-la-Neuve: Université Catholique de Louvain.

Gordon, D.F. 1974: A neo-classical theory of Keynesian unemployment. *Economic Inquiry*, 12, 431–59.

Greenberg, J. 1977: Quasi equilibrium in abstract economies without ordered preferences. *Journal of Mathematical Economics*, 4, 163–65.

Greenberg, J. and Müller, H. 1979: Equilibria under price rigidities and externalities. In O. Moeschlin and D. Pallaschke (eds), *Game Theory and Related Topics*, Amsterdam: North-Holland, 291–300.

Grossman, S.J. and Hart, O.D. 1979: A theory of competitive equilibrium in stock-market economies. *Econometrica*, 47, 293–330.

Grossman, S.J. and Hart, O.D. 1983: Implicit contracts under asymmetric information. *Quarterly Journal of Economics* (supplement) 71, 113–57.

Guesnerie, R. and de Montbrial, T. 1974: Allocation under uncertainty: a survey. Chapter 4 in Drèze (1974a).

Hart, O.D. 1983: Optimal labour contracts under asymmetric information: an introduction. *Review of Economic Studies*, 3–35.

Hart, O.D. and Holmström, B. 1988: The theory of contracts. In T. Bewley (ed.), *Advances in Economic Theory*, Cambridge: Cambridge University Press, 71–155.

Hirshleifer, J. and Riley, J.G. 1979: The analytics of uncertainty and information: an expository survey. *Journal of Economic Literature*, 17, 1375–421.

Holmström, B. 1983: Equilibrium long-term labour contracts. *Quarterly Journal of Economics* (supplement) 98, 23–54.

Ito, T. 1982: Implicit contract theory: a critical survey. Discussion paper 82–164, Center of Economic Research, University of Minnesota.

Jensen, M. and Meckling, W. 1979: Rights and production functions: an application to labour-managed firms and codetermination. *Journal of Business*, 52, 4, 469–506.

Laakkonen, V. 1977: *The Cooperative Movement in Finland 1945–1974*, Helsinki: Painosavolainen.

Lange, O. 1938: On the economic theory of socialism. In B.E. Lippincott (ed.), *On the Economic Theory of Socialism*, Minneapolis: University of Minnesota Press, 57–143 (second printing 1948).

Leroy, R. 1983: *Un scénario égalitaire*, Louvain-la-Neuve: CIACO.

Lindbeck, A. and Snower, D. 1985: Explanations of unemployment. *Oxford Review of Economic Policy*, 1, 2, 34–59.

Maddison, A. 1982: *Phases of Capitalist Development*, Oxford: Oxford University Press.

Malinvaud, E. 1971: A planning approach to the public good problem. *The Swedish Journal of Economics*, 73, 96–112.

Malinvaud, E. 1977: *The Theory of Unemployment Reconsidered*. Oxford: Basil Blackwell.

Meade, J.E. 1972: The theory of labour-managed firms and profit sharing. *Economic Journal*, 82, 402–28.

Meade, J.E. 1974: Labour-managed firms in conditions of imperfect competition. *Economic Journal*, 84, 817–24.

Meade, J.E. 1982: *Wage Fixing*, London: Allen.

Milleron, C. 1972: Theory of value with public goods: a survey article. *Journal of Economic Theory*, 5, 419–77.

Miyazaki, H. and Neary, H.N. 1983: The Illyrian firm revisited. *Bell Journal of Economics*, 14, 259–70.

Modigliani, F. and Pogue, G.A. 1974: An introduction to risk and return. *Financial Analysts Journal*, March, 68–80; April, 69–86.

Mossin, J. 1977: *The Economic Efficiency of Financial Markets*. Lexington, Mass.: Heath.

Newbery, D.M.G. and Stiglitz, J.E. 1979: Share-cropping, risk-sharing and the importance of imperfect information. In *Risk and Uncertainty in Agricultural Development*, Agricultural Development Council, New York, 311–41.

Oakeshott, R. 1973: Mondragon: Spain's oasis of democracy. *Observer*, 23 January 1973: chapter 19 in Vanek (1975).

Peters, M. 1983: Labour contracts in a stock-market economy. *Journal of Economic Theory*, 30, 296–314.

Pratt, J.W. 1964: Risk aversion in the small and in the large. *Econometrica*, 32, 122–66.

Radner, R. 1982: Equilibrium under uncertainty. Chapter 20 in K.J. Arrow and M.D. Intriligator (eds). *Handbook of Mathematical Economics*, Amsterdam: North-Holland.

Rosen, S. 1985: Implicit contracts: a survey. *Journal of Economic Literature*, 23, 3, 1144–75.

Sapir, A. 1980: A growth model for a tenured labour-managed firm. *Quarterly Journal of Economics*, 95, 3, 387–402.

Shafer, W. and Sonneschein, H. 1975: Equilibrium in abstract economies without ordered preferences. *Journal of Mathematical Economics*, 2, 345–8.

Spinnewyn, F. 1981: Labour-managed firms, profit-sharing and lay offs. Leuven: Katholieke Universiteit Leuven.

Steinherr, A. 1977: On the efficiency of profit-sharing and labour participation in management. *The Bell Journal of Economics*, 8, 543–55.

Steinherr, A. and Thisse, J.F. 1979: Are labour managers really perverse? *Economics Letters*, 2, 137–42.

Steinherr, A. and Vanek, J. 1976: Labour-managed firms in conditions of imperfect competition: a comment. *Economic Journal*, 86, 339–41.

Stiglitz, J.E. 1974: Incentives and risk-sharing in share-cropping. *Review of Economic Studies*, 41, 219–55.

Svejnar, J. 1982: On the theory of a participatory firm. *Journal of Economic Theory*, 27, 2, 313–30.

Vanek, J. 1970: *General Theory of Labour-Managed Market Economies*. Ithaca: Cornell University Press.

Vanek, J. 1971: The basic theory of financing of participatory firms. Department of Economics Working Paper. Ithaca: Cornell University. Reprinted in Vanek 1975.

Vanek, J. (ed.) 1975: *Self Management: economic liberation of man*, Harmondsworth: Penguin.

Vanek, J. and Jovicic, M. 1975: The capital and income distribution in Yugoslavia. *Quarterly Journal of Economics*, 89, 432–43.

Ward, B. 1958: The firm in Illyria: market syndicalism. *American Economic Review*, 68, 566–89.

Weitzman, M.L. 1984: *The Share Economy: conquering stagflation*. Cambridge, Mass.: Harvard University Press.

Wilson, R. 1968: On the theory of syndicates. *Econometrica*, 36, 119–32.

Index

Numbers in italic refer to entries in the References section.